Hugo's Simplified System

French in
Three Months

Hugo's Language Books Ltd, London

This edition 1987
© 1986 Hugo's Language Books Ltd
ISBN 0 85285 097 2

Written by

Ronald Overy
F.I.L.

Senior Lecturer
Department of Modern Languages
South Bank Polytechnic

Jacqueline Lecanuet
L. ès L., PG Dip. Ling.

Senior Lecturer and Head of French
Department of Modern Languages
South Bank Polytechnic

Set in 10/12 Plantin by
Phoenix Photosetting and
Reproduced, printed and bound in Great Britain by
Hazell Watson & Viney Limited,
Member of the BPCC Group,
Aylesbury, Bucks

Preface

This new edition of 'French in Three Months' has been written for us by two Polytechnic lecturers, whose combined experience in teaching French ranges from beginners to post-graduate level.

Ronald Overy is a Fellow of the Institute of Linguists and the author of French, Spanish and Russian textbooks. Jacqueline Lecanuet is a graduate of Caen and Lille Universities and holds a post-graduate diploma in linguistics.

The book begins with an explanation of French pronunciation, as far as this is possible in print. If you are working without a teacher, you will find that our system of 'imitated pronunciation' simplifies matters considerably. Using the book together with our cassette recordings is an ideal combination and provides another dimension to the course.

It has always been a principle of the Hugo method to teach only what is really essential. We assume that the student wants to learn French from a practical angle; the lessons contain those rules of grammar that will be of most use in this respect. Constructions are clearly explained, and the order in which everything is presented takes into consideration the need for rapid progress. Each lesson includes a large number of exercises and the vocabulary introduced is both practical and up-to-date. Often, in addition to testing a grammatical point, an exercise will include a specific vocabulary, for example: Exercise 45 deals with relative pronouns and the hotel, Exercise 57 with conjunctions and camping, Exercise 67 with the subjunctive and space travel. The Conversations offer examples of everyday French and frequently contain a touch of humour.

The course finishes with a short selection of reading passages illustrating both literary and journalistic styles, all with an English translation. It is important to remember, however, that idiomatic language cannot be translated literally without the occasional appearance of some rather stilted phrases.

Ideally, you should spend about an hour a day on your work (slightly less, maybe, if you do not use the cassette recordings), although there is no hard and fast rule on this. Do as much as you feel capable of doing; if you have no special aptitude for language-learning, there is no point in forcing yourself beyond your daily capacity to assimilate new material. It is much better to learn a little at a time, and to learn that thoroughly.

Before beginning a new section or lesson, always spend ten minutes revising what you learnt the day before. When studying the lessons, first read each rule or numbered section carefully and re-read it to ensure that you have fully understood the grammar, then translate the following exercise(s) by writing down the answers. Check these by referring to the Key at the back of the book; if you have made too many mistakes, go back over the instruction before attempting the same questions again. After you have listened to the Conversations, read them aloud and see how closely you can imitate the voices on the recording.

When the course is completed, you should have a very good understanding of the language – more than sufficient for general holiday or business purposes, and enough to lead quickly into an examination syllabus if this is your eventual aim. Remember that it is important to continue expanding your vocabulary through reading, listening to the radio, and best of all, through visiting the country.

We hope you will enjoy 'French in Three Months', and we wish you success with your studies.

Contents

6

Pronunciation

French is a very pleasant sounding language, but it can present one or two problems from the point of view of pronunciation. We have, however, simplified the whole question by using Hugo's method of imitated pronunciation, which is sufficiently accurate to make yourself understood. Naturally, if you wish to hear perfect pronunciation, you should acquire the cassette recordings which we have produced to accompany the course; these tapes allow you to hear the words and phrases as you follow them in the book.

Although French spelling appears complicated, it still remains more phonetic than that of English.

You should read through the following rules and advice on French pronunciation, but there is no need to learn the rules by heart; just refer back to them at frequent intervals and you will soon become familiar with them. In the meantime, you can start at Lesson 1 and rely on our imitated pronunciation.

Stress

Unlike English, all syllables in French words are distinctly sounded and evenly stressed, with a little more emphasis being given to the last syllable. Contrast the stress in the word 'important' which appears in both languages:

English: im-POR-tant
French: ang-por-tahng

Pronunciation of vowels

a   is pronounced like 'ah' in English: la (the).
à   is also pronounced like 'ah': là (there).
â   is pronounced like 'ah' but longer: âne (donkey).
e   is pronounced like ai in 'fair' in the middle of a syllable: mer (sea).

e	is pronounced like er in 'her' at the end of a syllable: le (the).
e	is silent at the end of a word: tasse (cup).
é	is pronounced like 'ay': été (summer).
è	is pronounced like ai in 'fair': père (father).
ê	is also pronounced like ai in 'fair': tête (head).
i,y	are pronounced like ee in 'meet': ski (skiing), y (there).
o	is pronounced like o in 'not': poste (post office).
ô	is pronounced like 'oh': hôtel.
u	this sound does not exist in English; say 'ee' with rounded lips: vu (seen).
oi	is pronounced like 'wah': roi (king).
ou	is pronounced like 'oo': roue (wheel).
ai,ei	are pronounced like e in 'let': laine (wool), reine (queen).
au,eau	are pronounced like 'oh': au (to the), eau (water).
eu,oeu	are pronounced like er in 'her': neuf (nine), soeur (sister).

Pronunciation of consonants

French consonants are pronounced as in English, but note the following:

c	before e or i sounds like 's': ceci (this).
c	elsewhere sounds like 'k': car (coach).
ç	sounds like 's': ça (that).
ch	sounds like 'sh': château (castle).
g	before e or i sounds like s in 'measure': général.
g	elsewhere sounds like g in 'go': gare (station).
h	is silent: hôtel.
j	sounds like s in 'measure': je (I).
qu,q	sound like 'k': qui (who).
r	is pronounced at the back of the throat; it is the sound we make when gargling: rire (to laugh).
s	at the beginning of a word sounds like 's': salle (room).
s	between two vowels sounds like 'z': rose.

IMPORTANT: with the exception of c, f, l and r, consonants are not usually pronounced when they form the last letter of a word:

passepor*t*, Pari*s*   BUT   hote*l*, professeu*r*

Nasal sounds

These sounds are very characteristic of the French language, but we have nasal sounds in English too: compare: sing, sang, sung, song – remembering that the standard pronunciation gives very little value to the g. In French there are four very similar nasal sounds:

om,on pronounce like ong in 'song': nom (name), non (no).

um*,un pronounce like ung in 'sung': un (one), brun (brown).

am,an, pronounce like 'ahng': champ (field), an (year),
em,en temps (time), en (in).

im*,in, pronounce like ang in 'sang': simple (easy), vin (wine),
aim,ain, faim (hunger), bain (bath),
ein plein (full).

ien pronounce like 'ee-ang': bien (well).

*Some French speakers make no distinction between these two sounds and pronounce them both like ang in 'sang'.

Variations

er at the end of a word of two syllables or more sounds like 'ay': parler (to speak).
ez at the end of a word sounds like 'ay': nez (nose).
ail at the end of a word sounds like 'ah'ee': travail (work).
eil,eille sound like 'ay'ee': soleil (sun), bouteille (bottle).
ill usually sounds like 'ee'y': billet (bee-yay, ticket).
gn sounds like ni in 'onion': signal.

Liaison

The French like their language to flow smoothly. For this reason, if a word beginning with a vowel or a silent h follows a word ending in a consonant, this consonant is linked to the beginning of the second word:

nous avons (noo zah-vong), we have
un petit enfant (ung p'tee tahng-fahng), a small child

When carried over in this way,

s,x   sound like 'z': deux ans (der zah*ng*), two years.

d   sounds like 't': un grand arbre (u*ng* grah*ng* tahbr), a tall tree.

f   sounds like 'v': neuf heures (ner ver*r*), nine hours.

Accents

There are three accents in French:

the acute (´), found on the letter e;
the grave (`), found on a, e and u;
the circumflex (^), found on any vowel.

There is also the cedilla (ˎ), found only underneath the letter c.

The function of the accents is:

a) to modify the sound of a letter. The unaccented e sounds like er in 'her', the é acute sounds like ay in 'say' and the è grave sounds like ai in 'fair'.

The c which would be hard before an a or o (as in 'car') is softened to sound like s in 'sit' when it has a cedilla added (garçon).

b) to distinguish between words having the same spelling but a different meaning. For example, la (the), là (there); ou (or), où (where); sur (on), sûr (sure).

The Imitated Pronunciation

Pronounce all syllables as if they formed part of an English word, giving equal stress to each syllable, but note the following:

ng (italics)	must never be pronounced; these letters merely indicate that the preceding vowel has a nasal sound.
er (r italics)	do not pronounce the r; this syllable sounds like er in 'her'.
zh	sounds like s in 'measure'.
ü	no equivalent in English; round your lips and say 'ee'.
o	sounds like o in 'not'.
oh	sounds like o in 'note'.

The French alphabet

This is the same as in English, but F
should know how to pronounce the l
your name to a French receptionist
'ahsh ah el er ee-grek' will make se
would not.

A (ah)	H (ahsh)	O		
B (bay)	I (ee)	P		
C (say)	J (zhee)	Q		
D (day)	K (kah)	R (arr)	Y (ee-grek)	
E (er)	L (el)	S (ess)	Z (zed)	
F (ef)	M (em)	T (tay)		
G (zhay)	N (en)	U (ü)		

1 Articles

In French all nouns are either masculine or feminine and articles ('the', 'a', 'some') must agree in gender and number with the noun to which they refer.

'The' is expressed by:

le (*m.sing.*)   **le passeport** the passport
la (*f.sing.*)   **la cassette** the cassette
l' (before a vowel or h★)   **l'alcool** the alcohol, **l'hôtel** the hotel
les (*m.& f.pl.*)   **les passeports** the passports

★A few words beginning with h take **le, la.**

'A' is expressed by:

un (*m.sing.*)   **un chéquier** a cheque book
une (*f.sing.*)   **une cigarette** a cigarette

'Some' or 'any' is expressed by:

du (*m.sing.*)   **du vin** some wine
de la (*f.sing.*)   **de la bière** some beer
de l' (before a vowel or h)   **de l'alcool** some alcohol
des (*m.& f.pl.*)   **des cassettes** some cassettes

Note: **du** is actually a contraction of **de** and **le**, and **des** is a contraction of **de** and **les.**

Sometimes 'some' and 'any' are omitted in English, but they must always be expressed in French:

we have wine   **nous avons du vin**

IMITATED PRONUNCIATION (1): ler pahs-porr; lah kah-set; lahl-kol; loh-tel; lay pahs-porr; ung shek-yay; ün see-gah-ret; dü vang; der lah bee-airr; der lahl-kol; day kah-set; noo zah-vong dü vang.

2 Nouns

Unfortunately, there are few rules that can help to determine the gender of French nouns. The best rule of all is to learn each noun and its gender together. Generally speaking, -e and -ion are feminine endings, although there are exceptions. Nouns denoting male persons are masculine and those which refer to female persons are feminine:

le monsieur gentleman
le journal newspaper
le parfum perfume
le magnétophone tape recorder
le château castle
le neveu nephew
le prix price
l'autobus (*m.*) bus

la dame lady
la valise suitcase
la station station

le journaliste male journalist
la journaliste female journalist

Occasionally only one gender exists and this has to be used irrespective of the sex of the person:

le professeur (teacher) is always masculine
la personne (person) is always feminine

IMITATED PRONUNCIATION (2): mers-yer; zhoor-nahl; pahr-fung; man-yay-to-fon; shah-toh; ner-ver; pree; oh-toh-büs; dahm; vah-leez; stahs-yong; zhoor-nah-leest; pro-fess-err; pairr-sonn.

2a Plural of nouns

The plural is formed:

a) by adding **s**

   magnétophone (tape recorder) becomes **magnétophones**
b) by adding **x** to words ending in **au** or **eu**

   château (castle) becomes **châteaux**
   neveu (nephew) becomes **neveux**

c) by changing the ending **al** to **aux**

    journal (newspaper) becomes **journaux**

Words ending in **s** and **x** do not change: **autobus** (bus *or* buses); **prix** (price *or* prices).

IMITATED PRONUNCIATION (2a): man-yay-to-fon; shah-toh; ner-ver; zhoor-nahl; zhoor-noh; oh-toh-büs; pree.

Exercise 1

Translate:
1 the passport
2 the hotel
3 the suitcase
4 a station
5 a tape recorder
6 a cheque book
7 a person
8 the journalists
9 the prices
10 some beer
11 some wine
12 some cassettes
13 some newspapers
14 some buses

3 Subject pronouns

singular		*plural*	
je	I	**nous**	we
tu	you (*familiar*)	**vous**	you (*familiar*)
vous	you (*formal*)	**vous**	you (*formal*)
il	he, it (*m.*)	**ils**	they (*m.*)
elle	she, it (*f.*)	**elles**	they (*f.*)

Note: je becomes j' before a vowel or h.

3a Forms of Address

English, on occasions, can be a very straightforward language. Whether we are addressing a dog, our husband or wife, or the Prime Minister, we use the same word 'you'. In French, it's not quite so simple because we have two words for 'you' – **tu** and **vous** – and to use them incorrectly would be a very serious mistake.

The French use **tu** when talking to animals, children, very close friends and relatives. Note, however, that although you use **tu** to one child, you would address more than one child as **vous**. Teenagers use **tu** to each other even on the first meeting.

In all other cases we use the more formal **vous**. Unless we indicate otherwise (by putting in brackets the word 'familiar') we would like you to use **vous** in all the exercises in this book.

Note also that what has been said about **tu** and **vous** also applies to **te** (you), **ton** (your), **votre** (your) etc.

You are no doubt already vaguely familiar with the words **Monsieur**, **Madame** and **Mademoiselle**; they mean Mr, Mrs and Miss and are placed, as in English, before a surname:

Monsieur Dupont, Madame Duval, Mademoiselle Martin.

The French also use these words a great deal in formal conversation, without a name following:

Bonjour, Monsieur.   Good morning, good afternoon (to a man).
Bonsoir, Madame.   Good evening (to a woman).
Au revoir, Mademoiselle.   Goodbye (to a young woman).

Monsieur, Madame and **Mademoiselle** also have a plural form:
Messieurs, Mesdames, Mesdemoiselles.

IMITATED PRONUNCIATION (3, 3a): zher; tü; voo; eel; el; noo; voo; voo; eel, el; mers-yer dü-pong; mah-dahm dü-vahl; mahd-mwah-zel mahr-tang; bong-zhoor, mers-yer; bong-swahr, mah-dahm; orr-vwahrr, mahd-mwah-zel; mays-yer; may-dahm; mayd-mwah-zel.

4 The verb 'avoir' (to have)

This is one of the most important French verbs and it should be learnt thoroughly.

Present tense

j'ai	I have
tu as	you have (*familiar sing.*)
il a, elle a	he has, she has
nous avons	we have
vous avez	you have (*formal, sing.* and *pl.*)
ils ont, elles ont	they (*m.*) have, they (*f.*) have

Vocabulary

Study these words:

le livre	book
l'appareil-photo (*m.*)	camera
le disque	record
la carte	map, card
la clé	key
la voiture	car
la radio	radio
oui	yes
non	no
et	and

IMITATED PRONUNCIATION (4): ah-vwahr; zhay; tü ah; eel ah; el ah; noo zah-vo*ng*; voo zah-vay; eel zo*ng*; el zo*ng*; leevr; ah-pah-ray'ee fo-toh; deesk; kahrt; klay; vwah-tür; rad-yoh; wee; no*ng*; ay.

Exercise 2

Answer the questions as follows:

Pierre a du vin?	Does Pierre have any wine?
Oui, il a du vin.	Yes, he has some wine.

1 Nicole a un journal?
2 Sophie et Pierre ont une voiture?
3 Vous avez une radio?
4 Vous avez une carte?
5 Nous avons une clé?
6 J'ai un disque?

Notice that we can ask questions simply by using a rising intonation.

5 The negative

'Not' is expressed by the two words ne . . . pas; ne is placed before the verb and pas after; ne becomes n' before a vowel or h:

je n'ai pas	I have not
il n'a pas	he has not
elle n'a pas	she has not
nous n'avons pas	we have not
vous n'avez pas	you have not (*formal, sing. and pl.*)
ils n'ont pas	they (*m.*) have not
elles n'ont pas	they (*f.*) have not

The singular familiar form **tu as** becomes **tu n'as pas.**

After a negative **un, une, du, de la, de l'** and **des** change to **de** (**d'** before a vowel or h).

J'ai de la bière.	I have some beer.
Je n'ai pas de bière.	I have no beer.

IMITATED PRONUNCIATION (5): zher nay pah; eel nah pah; el nah pah; noo nah-vong pah; voo nah-vay pah; eel nong pah; el nong pah; tü nah pah; zhay der lah bee-airr; zher nay pah der bee-airr.

Exercise 3

Answer the questions as follows:

Vous avez une voiture?   Do you have a car?
Non, je n'ai pas de voiture.   No, I don't have a car.

1 Vous avez une valise?
2 Vous avez un passeport?
3 Nous avons du vin?
4 Nous avons un livre?
5 Paul a des disques?
6 Anne-Marie a une radio?
7 J'ai des journaux?
8 Elles ont un appareil-photo?

Exercise 4

Translate:

1 I have a tape recorder.
2 I do not have any keys.
3 We have a suitcase.
4 She has some alcohol.
5 He does not have a newspaper.
6 They (*m.*) have some cassettes.
7 They (*f.*) do not have any maps.
8 You do not have a cheque book.
9 Do you have a camera?
10 Do you have any records?
11 Do you have any books?
12 Do you have a radio?

Vocabulary

à	at, to
au (à + le = au)	at the
le contrôle	control, check
le policier	policeman
le douanier	customs officer
l'instant (*m.*)	moment
le miracle	miracle
la douane	customs
le/la touriste	tourist
déclarer	to declare
c'est	this is, that is
s'il vous plaît	please
voici	here is, here are
où	where
très	very
grave	serious
quelque chose	something
mais	but
mon Dieu	good heavens
aussi	also

IMITATED PRONUNCIATION: ah; oh; ko*ng*-trohl; po-lees-yay;
dwahn-yay; a*ng*-stah*ng*; mee-rahkl; dwahn; too-reest; day-klah-ray;
say; seel voo play; vwah-see; oo; tray; grahv; kel-ke*r* shohz; may;
mo*ng* dye*r*; oh-see.

CONVERSATION

Au contrôle des passeports

Policier	Passeport, s'il vous plaît, Madame.
Touriste	Un instant, s'il vous plaît.
	(She searches in her handbag.)
	Le passeport? Où est le passeport? Mon Dieu!
	J'ai un chéquier, un livre, une carte de France, une cassette, des clés, des cigarettes mais . . . je n'ai pas de passeport!

À la douane

Douanier	Vous avez quelque chose à déclarer?
Touriste	Oui, je n'ai pas de passeport.
Douanier	Vous n'avez pas de passeport? C'est très grave. Vous avez de l'alcool?
Touriste	Oui, j'ai du vin.
Douanier	Vous avez du parfum?
Touriste	Non, je n'ai pas de parfum.
Douanier	Vous avez des cigarettes?
Touriste	Oui, j'ai des cigarettes. J'ai aussi un appareil-photo, un magnétophone et des cassettes.
	(The customs officer asks her to open the suitcase.)
Douanier	Voici le vin, voici le magnétophone, l'appareil-photo, les cassettes, les cigarettes, un journal, un livre et . . . miracle - voici le passeport!

TRANSLATION

At the Passport Control

Immigration Officer	Passport please, Madam.
Tourist	One moment, please.
	(She searches in her handbag.)
	The passport? Where's the passport? Good heavens! I have a cheque book, a book, a map of France, a cassette, some keys, some cigarettes but . . . I have no passport!

At the Customs

Customs Officer	Do you have anything to declare?
Tourist	Yes, I've no passport.
Customs Officer	You've no passport? That's very serious. Do you have any alcohol?
Tourist	Yes, I have some wine.
Customs Officer	Do you have any perfume?
Tourist	No, I haven't got any perfume.
Customs Officer	Do you have any cigarettes?
Tourist	Yes, I have some cigarettes. I also have a camera, a tape recorder and some cassettes.
	(*The customs officer asks her to open the suitcase.*)
Customs Officer	Here's the wine, here's the tape recorder, the camera, the cassettes, the cigarettes, a newspaper, a book and surprise, surprise . . . here's the passport!

Lesson 2

6 The verb 'être' (to be)

This is another very important verb and should be learned thoroughly.

Present tense

je suis	I am
tu es	you are (*familiar sing.*)
il est	he is
elle est	she is
nous sommes	we are
vous êtes	you are
ils sont	they are (*m.*)
elles sont	they are (*f.*)

IMITATED PRONUNCIATION (6): zher swee; tü ay; eel ay; el ay; noo som; voo zet; eel so*ng*; el so*ng*.

Vocabulary

Study these professions:

le médecin	doctor
le banquier	banker
le pilote	pilot
le professeur	teacher
l'avocat (*m.*)	lawyer
l'avocate (*f.*)	lawyer
l'hôtesse de l'air	air hostess
le/la journaliste	journalist
le/la secrétaire	secretary
l'astronaute (*m.* or *f.*)	astronaut

Note: when talking about their professions, the French omit the 'a' and say 'I am doctor', 'I am pilot' etc., **je suis médecin, je suis pilote.**

IMITATED PRONUNCIATION: med-sa*ng*; bah*ng*k-yay; pee-lot; pro-fess-e*rr*; ah-vo-kah; ah-vo-kaht; oh-tess-de*r*-lairr; zhoor-nah-leest; se*r*-kray-tairr; ah-stro-noht.

Exercise 5

Translate:
1 I am a doctor.
2 He is a pilot.
3 She is a journalist.
4 We are bankers.
5 You (*m.*) are a lawyer.
6 They are air hostesses.
7 They (*m.*) are astronauts.

7 Adjectives

French adjectives have both a masculine and a feminine form, singular and plural. The feminine is normally formed by adding **e** (those already ending in e do not change). In the plural we usually add **s**:

Il est intelligent.   He is intelligent.
Elle est intelligente.   She is intelligent.
Je suis grand.   I (*m.*) am tall.
Je suis grande.   I (*f.*) am tall.
Ils sont petits.   They (*m.*) are small.
Elles sont petites.   They (*f.*) are small.

Note: the addition of the **e** results in the preceding consonant being pronounced.

Adjectives ending in **x** change the **x** to **se** in the feminine:

dangereux dangerous, becomes **dangereuse**

IMITATED PRONUNCIATION (7): a*ng*-tel-ee-zhah*ng*; a*ng*-tel-ee-zhah*ng*t; grah*ng*; grah*ng*d; p'tee; p'teet; dah*ng*-zher-rer; dah*ng*-zher-rerz.

Vocabulary

riche	rich
pauvre	poor
facile	easy
difficile	difficult
intéressant	interesting
ennuyeux	boring
intelligent	intelligent
stupide	stupid
poli	polite
impoli	impolite
heureux	happy
malheureux	unhappy
bon, bonne (*f.*)	good
mauvais	bad

Additional rules for forming the feminine of adjectives:
a) final **f** changes to **ve: attentif, attentive** (*f.*) – attentive
b) final **er** changes to **ère: premier, première** (*f.*) – first
c) final **et** changes to **ète: secret, secrète** (*f.*) – secret

IMITATED PRONUNCIATION: reesh; pohvr; fah-seel; dee-fee-seel; ang-tay-ress-ahng; ahng-nwee-yer; ang-tel-ee-zhahng; stü-peed; po-lee; ang-po-lee; er-rer; mahl-er-rer; bong; bonn; moh-vay; ah-tahng-teef; ah-tahng-teev; prerm-yay; prerm-yairr; serkray; serkret.

Exercise 6

Give the opposite of:
1 Le banquier est riche.
2 La secrétaire est intelligente.
3 Les médecins sont heureux.
4 Les journaux sont intéressants.
5 Le vin est bon.
6 Le livre est facile.
7 L'hôtesse de l'air est polie.
8 La bière est mauvaise.

8 Regular verbs ending in -er

The infinitive of most French verbs ends in **-er**:

préparer	to prepare
habiter	to live
travailler	to work
parler	to speak
pratiquer	to practise
regarder	to watch
écouter	to listen (to)

We form the present tense by removing the **-er** from the infinitive and adding:

je	-e		**nous**	-ons
tu	-es		**vous**	-ez
il/elle	-e		**ils/elles**	-ent

je parle	I speak
tu parles	you speak (*fam.*)
il parle	he speaks
elle parle	she speaks
nous parlons	we speak
vous parlez	you speak
ils parlent	they speak (*m.*)
elles parlent	they speak (*f.*)

The French **je parle**, **il parle** etc. translates all three forms of the English present tense i.e. I speak, I do speak, I am speaking.

IMITATED PRONUNCIATION (8): pray-pah-ray; ah-bee-tay; trah-vah'ee-yay; pahr-lay; prah-tee-kay; rer-gahr-day; ay-koo-tay; zher pahrl; tü pahrl; eel pahrl; el pahrl; noo pahr-long; voo pahr-lay; eel pahrl; el pahrl.

Vocabulary

à	in, at
voyager	to travel
(**nous voyageons**; see section 81 for details of spelling changes.)	
le sport	sport
la langue	language
la télévision	television

la radio	radio
l'enquête (*f.*)	survey
deux	two

IMITATED PRONUNCIATION:ah; vwah-yah-zhay; sporr; lah*ng*g; tay-lay-vee-zee-o*ng*; rahd-yoh; ah*ng*-ket; de*r*.

Exercise 7

Complete these sentences:
1 Nous (live) à Versailles.
2 Elle (works) à Nice.
3 Il (travels).
4 Je (speak) deux langues.
5 Elles (practise) un sport.
6 Ils (watch) la télévision.
7 Vous (listen to) la radio.
8 Nous (prepare) une enquête.

9 The interrogative

In French you can ask a question:

(a) by using a rising intonation. Contrast:

Vous parlez français. You speak French. (statement)
Vous parlez français? Do you speak French? (question)

(b) by using **est-ce que** (**est-ce qu'** before a vowel or h):

Est-ce que nous travaillons? Are we working?
Est-ce qu'elle écoute la radio? Is she listening to the radio?

(c) by putting the pronoun after the verb:

Voyagez-vous beaucoup? Do you travel a great deal?

A **t** is inserted in the third person singular if it ends in a vowel:

Fume-t-il? Does he smoke?

Note: (a) and (b) are less formal than (c) and are used more in the spoken language.

Vocabulary

téléphoner	to telephone
réserver	to reserve
exporter	to export
importer	to import
voter	to vote
inviter à dîner	to invite to dinner
il y a	there is, there are
l'hôtel (*m.*)	hotel
le directeur	director
l'ordinateur (*m.*)	computer
le premier ministre	Prime Minister
l'agent (*m.*)	agent
le mousquetaire	musketeer
le pays	country
le marché	market
juillet (*m.*)	July
la chambre	bedroom
la voiture	car
la date	date
la prise	taking, storming
la Bastille	Bastille
secret	secret
commun	common
finalement	finally
dans	in
de	of
en France	in France, to France

IMITATED PRONUNCIATION (9): frah*ng*-say; ess-ker; boh-koo; füm-teel;
tay-lay-fo-nay; ray-zairr-vay; eks-porr-tay; a*ng*-porr-tay; vo-tay;
a*ng*-vee-tay ah dee-nay; eel yah; oh-tel; dee-rek-terr; orr-dee-nah-terr;
pre*rm*-yay mee-neestr; ah-zhah*ng*; moo-sker-tairr; pay-ee;
mahr-shay; zhwee-yay; shah*ng*br; vwah-tür; daht; preez; bah-stee-y;
ser-kray; ko-mu*ng*; fee-nahl-mah*ng*; dah*ng*; der; ah*ng* frah*ng*s.

Exercise 8

Using est-ce que, ask your friend whether he/she . . .

1 is telephoning the hotel. (say *to* the hotel)
2 is reserving a room.
3 is inviting the director to dinner.

Using a rising intonation, ask about Nicole . . .

4 Is she intelligent?
5 Is she interesting?
6 Is she tall?

Using the inverted form, ask about Peter . . .

7 Does he export computers to France?
8 Does he import cars?
9 Does he vote for the Prime Minister?

10 Numerals

Here are the numbers 0 – 15

0	**zéro**	8	**huit**
1	**un**	9	**neuf**
2	**deux**	10	**dix**
3	**trois**	11	**onze**
4	**quatre**	12	**douze**
5	**cinq**	13	**treize**
6	**six**	14	**quatorze**
7	**sept**	15	**quinze**

IMITATED PRONUNCIATION: zay-roh; u*ng*; der; trwah; kahtr; sa*ng*k; sees; set; weet, ne*r*f; dees; o*ng*z; dooz; trez; kah-torrz; ka*ng*z.

Exercise 9

Complete the following, writing the answers in words:

a	7 + 2 =		e	10 + 5 =
b	8 − 6 =		f	14 − 2 =
c	3 × 4 =		g	2 × 7 =
d	2 + 3 =		h	2 + 1 =

Complete the following as above:

1 Le premier ministre habite _____ Downing Street.
2 James Bond, agent secret _____ .
3 La date de la prise de la Bastille: le _____ juillet.
4 Les Trois Mousquetaires sont finalement _____ .
5 Il y a _____ pays dans le Marché commun.

Vocabulary

sur	on
pour	for
beaucoup	a great deal
seulement	only
souvent	often
jamais	never
plusieurs	several
anglais	English
le jogging	jogging
l'agence (*f.*)	agency
la publicité	advertising
la question	question
les affaires (*f.*)	business
faire	to do, to make

IMITATED PRONUNCIATION: sürr; poorr; boh-koo; serl-mah*ng*; soo-vah*ng*; zhah-may; plüz-yerr; ah*ng*-glay; zhog-i*ng*; ah-zhah*ng*s; pü-blee-see-tay; kest-yo*ng*; ah-fairr; fairr.

Note: except when we refer to the people of the country, adjectives denoting nationality do not take a capital letter; **un hôtel français, je parle anglais** *but* **les Français**, the French.

CONVERSATION

A French radio reporter is preparing a survey on the French. He's interviewing passers-by in the street . . .

Journaliste Pardon Madame, vous êtes Française?
Passante Oui, je suis Française.

Journaliste	Je prépare une enquête sur les Français. J'ai sept questions.
Passante	Oui.
Journaliste	Vous habitez à Paris?
Passante	Non, j'habite à Versailles.
Journaliste	Vous travaillez à Paris?
Passante	Oui, je travaille pour une agence de publicité.
Journaliste	Est-ce que vous voyagez beaucoup?
Passante	Oui, je voyage pour affaires.
Journaliste	Est-ce que vous parlez plusieurs langues?
Passante	Deux seulement, français et anglais.
Journaliste	Pratiquez-vous un sport?
Passante	Oui, je fais du jogging.
Journaliste	Regardez-vous la télévision?
Passante	Oui, souvent.
Journaliste	Vous écoutez la radio?
Passante	Jamais!

TRANSLATION

Journalist	Excuse me Madam, are you French?
Passer-by	Yes, I'm French.
Journalist	I'm preparing a survey on the French. I've seven questions.
Passer-by	Yes.
Journalist	Do you live in Paris?
Passer-by	No, I live in Versailles.
Journalist	Do you work in Paris?
Passer-by	Yes, I work for an advertising agency.
Journalist	Do you travel a great deal?
Passer-by	Yes, I travel on business.
Journalist	Do you speak several languages?
Passer-by	Only two, French and English.
Journalist	Do you practise a sport?
Passer-by	Yes, I jog.
Journalist	Do you watch television?
Passer-by	Yes, often.
Journalist	Do you listen to the radio?
Passer-by	Never!

Lesson 3

11 Regular verbs ending in -ir

The infinitive of a large number of French verbs ends in **-ir**:

finir	to finish
garantir	to guarantee
choisir	to choose
grossir	to put on weight
maigrir	to lose weight
remplir	to fill
réussir	to succeed

We form the present tense by removing the **-ir** from the infinitive and adding:

je	**-is**		**nous**	**-issons**
tu	**-is**		**vous**	**-issez**
il/elle	**-it**		**ils/elles**	**-issent**

je finis	I finish
tu finis	you finish
il finit	he finishes
elle finit	she finishes
nous finissons	we finish
vous finissez	you finish
ils finissent (*m.*)	they finish
elles finissent (*f.*)	they finish

Note: the singular familiar form **tu finis** ('you finish') should be used only to close friends, children and animals.

Vocabulary

le rapport	report
le magnétoscope	video recorder
le gâteau	cake

le verre   glass
l'occasion (*f.*)   opportunity
saisir   to seize

IMITATED PRONUNCIATION (11): fee-neerr; gah-rah*ng*-teerr; shwah-zeerr; groh-seerr; may-greerr; rah*ng*-pleerr; ray-ü-seerr; fee-nee; fee-nee; fee-nee; fee-nee-so*ng*; fee-nee-say; fee-neess; rah-porr; man-yay-to-skop; gah-toh; vairr; o-kahz-yo*ng*; say-zeerr.

Exercise 10

Translate:
1 I am finishing the report.
2 We guarantee the video recorder.
3 She chooses a cake.
4 He is putting on weight.
5 They (*f.*) are losing weight.
6 They (*m.*) are filling the glasses.
7 We seize the opportunity.

12 Demonstrative adjectives

Both 'this' and 'that' are expressed by:

ce (*m. s.*)
cet (*m. s.*) before a vowel or h
cette (*f. s.*)

ce train this train
cet hélicoptère this helicopter
cette voiture that car

Both 'these' and 'those' are expressed by:

ces (*m. & f. pl.*)   **ces avions** these planes

If a distinction needs to be made between 'this' and 'that' or 'these' and 'those', we can add **-ci** (short for **ici** 'here') and **-là** ('there') to the noun:

ce train-ci   this train
ce train-là   that train

32

Vocabulary

le guichet	ticket office
l'ascenseur (*m.*)	lift
le compartiment	compartment
le billet	ticket
la gare	railway station
la place	seat
rapide	fast
important	important
fermé	closed
cher, chère (*f.*)	expensive
plein	full
réservé	reserved
occupé	occupied
valable	valid

IMITATED PRONUNCIATION (12): se*r* tra*ng*; set ay-lee-kop-tairr; set
vwah-türr; say zahv-yo*ng*; gee-shay; ah-sah*ng*-se*rr*;
ko*ng*-pahr-tee-mah*ng*; bee-yay; gahr; plahs; rah-peed; a*ng*-por-tah*ng*;
fairr-may; shairr; pla*ng*; ray-zairr-vay; o-kü-pay; vah-lahbl.

Exercise 11

Translate:
1 This train is fast.
2 This station is important.
3 This ticket office is closed.
4 That car is expensive.
5 That lift is full.
6 These seats are reserved.
7 These compartments are occupied.
8 Those tickets are valid.

13 Expressions with 'avoir' (to have)

In French there are a number of expressions with avoir 'to have'
which would be expressed in English with 'to be':

avoir faim	to be hungry
avoir soif	to be thirsty

avoir chaud	to be warm
avoir froid	to be cold
avoir raison	to be right
avoir tort	to be wrong

avoir is also used in connection with age:

Il a douze ans. He is twelve. (lit. 'He has twelve years').

IMITATED PRONUNCIATION: ah-vwahr fa*ng*; swahf; shoh; frwah; ray-zo*ng*; torr; ah*ng*.

Exercise 12

Give the opposite of:
1 J'ai faim
2 Il a raison.
3 Elle a chaud.
4 Nous avons soif.
5 Ils ont tort.
6 Elles ont froid.

14 Negatives

We have already seen that 'not' is expressed by putting **ne** (**n'**) before the verb and **pas** after:

Je ne travaille pas.   I do not work.
Il n'écoute pas.   He is not listening.

Here are some more negatives:

ne . . . . . jamais	never
ne . . . . . rien	nothing
ne . . . . . personne	no-one
ne . . . . . plus	no longer, no more

Examples:

Il ne travaille jamais.   He never works.
Elle n'exporte rien.   She exports nothing.
Ils n'invitent personne.   They invite no-one.
Je ne fume plus.   I no longer smoke.

Note:

a) **rien** and **personne** can also begin a sentence:
   Rien n'est cher. Nothing is expensive.
   Personne ne fume ici. No one smokes here.

b) after a negative **un, une, du, de la, de l', des** change to **de (d')**:
   Je mange de la salade. I eat salad.
   Je ne mange jamais de salade. I never eat salad.

Vocabulary

l'électrophone (*m.*)	record player
le fromage	cheese
l'homme d'affaires (*m.*)	businessman
la glace	ice cream
la diététicienne	dietician
manger	to eat
rencontrer	to meet
en	in, by

IMITATED PRONUNCIATION (14): ner; zhah-may; ree-a*ng*; pairr-sonn; plü; ay-lek-tro-fon; fro-mahzh; om dah-fairr; glahs; dyay-tay-tees-yen; mah*ng*-zhay; rah*ng*-ko*ng*-tray.

Exercise 13

Answer the questions using 'not', as follows:

Vous voyagez en voiture?   Do you travel by car?
Non, je ne voyage pas en voiture.   No, I don't travel by car.

1 Vous travaillez?
2 Vous écoutez?
3 Vous avez faim?

Now answer using 'never':

4 Est-ce que vous choisissez du fromage?
5 Est-ce que vous téléphonez?
6 Est-ce que vous avez froid?

Now answer using 'nothing':

7 Mange-t-il une glace?

8 Prépare-t-elle un rapport?
9 Exporte-t-il des électrophones?

Now answer using 'no-one':

10 Nous invitons des hommes d'affaires?
11 Nous choisissons Paul?
12 Nous rencontrons la diététicienne?

Now answer using 'no longer':

13 Est-ce qu'ils ont une voiture?
14 Est-ce qu'elles habitent à Paris?
15 Est-ce qu'elles travaillent?

15 Interrogatives

You will need to know how to ask questions in French:

où?   where?
Où est-ce que vous habitez?   Where do you live?

quand?   when?
Quand écoutez-vous la radio?   When do you listen to the radio?

comment?   how?
Comment allez-vous?   How are you? (literally: How do you go?)

qui?   who?   whom?
Qui parle français?   Who speaks French?
Qui est-ce qu'elle invite?   Whom is she inviting?

pourquoi?   why?
Pourquoi téléphone-t-elle?   Why is she telephoning?

Note: the reply to **pourquoi** is **parce que** 'because'.

quel (*m.*), **quelle** (*f.*)
quels (*m. pl.*), **quelles** (*f. pl.*)   which, what
Quelle chambre réservons-nous?   Which room are we reserving?

combien?   how much?   how many?
Combien coûte ce disque?   How much does this record cost?
Combien de fromage désirez-vous?   How much cheese do you want?

Combien de trains y a-t-il? How many trains are there?

Note: **combien** takes **de** (**d'**) when followed by a noun.

que (**qu'** before a vowel) or **qu'est-ce que**   what
Que mangez-vous? or **Qu'est-ce que vous mangez?**   What are you eating?

Note the word order in the above two questions.

Vocabulary

le film	film
le soir	evening
le franc	franc
allemand	German
espagnol	Spanish
bien	well
merci	thank you
chercher	to look for

IMITATED PRONUNCIATION (15): oo; kah*ng*; ko-mah*ng*; ko-mah*ng* tah-lay voo; kee; poorr-kwah; pahr-sker; kel; ko*ng*-bee-a*ng*; koot; deesk; day-zee-ray voo; yah-teel; ker; kess-ker; mah*ng*-zhay; feelm; swahr; frah*ng*; ahl-mah*ng*; ess-pan-yol; bee-a*ng*; mairr-see; shairr-shay.

Exercise 14

Below are ten replies. What were the questions? The important words are printed in italics.

1 Je travaille *à Paris*.
2 Je regarde le film *ce soir*.
3 *Bien*, merci.
4 *Pierre* téléphone.
5 Ils cherchent *Nicole*.
6 Parce que *j'ai faim*.
7 Je parle *espagnol et allemand*.
8 J'ai *quatre* cassettes.
9 Ce journal coûte *six francs*.
10 J'exporte *des magnétoscopes*.

16 The imperative

On occasions you will need to ask or tell people to do things. Simply omit the **vous, tu** or **nous** from the present tense:

Téléphonez.	Telephone.
Choisissez.	Choose.
Invitons Paul.	Let's invite Paul.
Ne téléphonez pas.	Don't telephone.
N'invitons pas Paul.	Let's not invite Paul.

Note: the final **s** of **-er** verbs is dropped in the familiar singular imperative:

Choisis.	Choose.
Finis.	Finish.
Téléphone.	Telephone.

You may wish to add **s'il vous plaît** or **s'il te plaît** (fam. sing.) 'please' to the imperative.

Vocabulary

les bagages (*m.*)	luggage
la méthode	method
trop	too much, too many
monter	to bring up, to take up
acheter	to buy

Note: in the present tense of the verb **acheter** a grave accent is introduced in the singular and in the third person plural. This affects the pronunciation; a more detailed explanation of it all will be found in section 81 'Spelling changes':

j'achète	**nous achetons**
tu achètes	**vous achetez**
il achète	
elle achète	
ils achètent	
elles achètent	

IMITATED PRONUNCIATION (16): bah-gahzh; may-tod; troh; mong-tay; ahsh-tay; zhah-shet; tü ah-shet; eel ah-shet; el ah-shet; eel zah-shet; el zah-shet; noo zahsh-tong; voo zahsh-tay.

Exercise 15

Tell your friend . . .

1 . . . to reserve two rooms.
2 . . . to look for François.
3 . . . to seize the opportunity.
4 . . . to choose the Hugo method.
5 . . . to take up the luggage.

Tell your friend . . .

6 . . . not to eat too much.
7 . . . not to put on weight.
8 . . . not to smoke.

And now make some suggestions:

9 Let's speak French.
10 Let's listen to the radio.
11 Let's finish the report.

Vocabulary

le régime	diet
l'interview (*f.*)	interview
la gymnastique	gymnastics, exercises
la chose	thing
la vie	life
penser	to think
je pense que	I think that
je dois	I must
faire	to do
(**vous faites**)	
raccourcir	to shorten
chaque	each
certain	certain
bien	good, fine (*as adverb*)
complètement	completely
régulièrement	regularly
toujours	always
entre	between
pour	for, in order to
bonjour	good morning, good afternoon

IMITATED PRONUNCIATION: ray-zheem; a*ng*-tairr-vyoo;
zheem-nah-steek; shohz; vee; pah*ng*-say; zhe*r* pah*ng*s ke*r*; zhe*r* dwah;
fairr; voo fet; rah-koor-seerr; shahk; sairr-ta*ng*; bee-a*ng*;
ko*ng*-plet-mah*ng*; ray-gül-yairr-mah*ng*; too-zhoorr; ah*ng*tr; poorr;
bo*ng*-zhoorr.

CONVERSATION

Une interview entre un homme d'affaires et une diététicienne.

Homme d'affaires	Bonjour, Madame.
Diététicienne	Bonjour, Monsieur. Un petit instant, s'il vous plaît, je finis ce rapport. Bon. Comment allez-vous?
Homme d'affaires	Je pense que je grossis.
Diététicienne	Ah? Vous ne réussissez pas à maigrir? Pourquoi pas?
Homme d'affaires	J'ai toujours faim. J'ai toujours soif. Qu'est-ce que je dois faire?
Diététicienne	Faites votre gymnastique régulièrement. Saisissez chaque occasion pour manger de la salade.
Homme d'affaires	Et qu'est-ce que je ne dois pas faire?
Diététicienne	Ne choisissez jamais de gâteaux. Ne choisissez jamais de glaces. Ne choisissez jamais de fromage.
Homme d'affaires	Très bien. Et pour le vin?
Diététicienne	Ne remplissez jamais votre verre complètement.
Homme d'affaires	Vous garantissez ce régime, Madame?
Diététicienne	Oui. Une chose est certaine: si vous grossissez, vous raccourcissez votre vie.
Homme d'affaires	Oui, Madame, vous avez raison.

TRANSLATION

An interview between a businessman and a dietician.

Businessman	Good morning, (Madam).
Dietician	Good morning, (Sir). One moment, please, I'll just finish (literally I finish) this report. Good. How are you?
Businessman	I think that I'm putting on weight.
Dietician	Oh? You're not managing to slim? Why not?
Businessman	I'm always hungry. I'm always thirsty. What must I do?
Dietician	Do your exercises regularly. Seize every opportunity to eat salad.
Businessman	And what must I not do?
Dietician	Never choose cakes. Never choose ice cream. Never choose cheese.
Businessman	Fine. And what about wine?
Dietician	Never fill your glass completely.
Businessman	Do you guarantee this diet, (Madam)?
Dietician	Yes. One thing is certain: if you put on weight, you shorten your life.
Businessman	Yes, (Madam). You're right.

Lesson 4

17 The perfect tense

You will often wish to talk about things that you have done. The French perfect tense translates all three forms of the English past: 'I have spoken', 'I did speak', 'I spoke'.

To form the perfect tense we:
a) change the **-er** of the infinitive into **-é**
b) change the **-ir** of the infinitive into **-i**:

Verbs ending in **-er**	Verbs ending in **-ir**
j'ai parlé	**j'ai fini**
tu as préparé	**tu as garanti**
il a habité	**il a choisi**
elle a travaillé	**elle a grossi**
nous avons regardé	**nous avons maigri**
vous avez écouté	**vous avez saisi**
ils ont voyagé	**ils ont raccourci**
elles ont téléphoné	**elles ont rempli**

Vocabulary

le document	document
l'Italie (*f.*)	Italy
la Manche	Channel
copier	to copy
dépenser	to spend (money)
passer	to spend (time)
traverser	to cross

IMITATED PRONUNCIATION (17): pahr-lay; pray-pah-ray; ah-bee-tay; etc., fee-nee; gah-rah*ng*-tee; shwah-zee; etc., do-kü-mah*ng*; ee-tah-lee; mah*ng*sh; kop-yay; day-pah*ng*-say; pah-say; trah-vairr-say.

Exercise 16

Translate:
1 I have lived in France.
2 I have worked in Italy.
3 I have reserved the rooms.
4 She listened to the radio.
5 She watched the television.
6 She prepared the report.
7 He has put on weight.
8 He has chosen the cheese.
9 He has finished the book.
10 We copied the document.
11 We bought the car.
12 We telephoned.
13 You guaranteed the tape recorder.
14 You seized the opportunity.
15 You invited the Prime Minister.
16 They (*m.*) have lost weight.
17 They (*f.*) have spent 15 francs.
18 They (*f.*) have crossed the Channel.

18 The perfect tense (negative)

You will also wish to say what you have *not* done:

je n'ai pas copié
tu n'as pas traversé
il n'a pas passé
elle n'a pas acheté
nous n'avons pas invité
vous n'avez pas garanti
ils n'ont pas rempli
elles n'ont pas fini

Note the position of **pas**

Exercise 17

Answer the questions as follows:

Avez-vous travaillé en Italie?   Have you worked in Italy?
Non, je n'ai pas travaillé en Italie.   No, I have not worked in Italy.

1 Avez-vous réservé la chambre?
2 Avez-vous écouté le disque?
3 A-t-il regardé le film?
4 A-t-elle préparé le document?
5 Est-ce que nous avons fini?
6 Est-ce qu'ils ont choisi?
7 Est-ce qu'elles ont mangé?

19 Possessive adjectives

It is important to be able to establish ownership:

	m.sing.	*f.sing.*	*m. & f. pl.*
my	mon	ma	mes
your (*fam.*)	ton	ta	tes
his/her/its	son	sa	ses
our	notre	notre	nos
your	votre	votre	vos
their	leur	leur	leurs

Note: these adjectives agree with the thing possessed, *not* with the possessor:

ma femme	my wife
son mari	her husband
votre chambre	you bedroom
nos clés	our keys
leurs disques	their records

Note also that if a feminine noun begins with a vowel, we write **mon, ton, son** *not* **ma, ta, sa**:

mon amie	my friend
ton agence	your agency
son enquête	his/her survey

This sounds more pleasant to the French ear.

Vocabulary

le vol	flight
l'horaire (*m.*)	timetable
la ceinture de sécurité	seat belt
la place	seat
attacher	to fasten, to attach
premier, première (*f.*)	first

IMITATED PRONUNCIATION (19): mong; mah; may; tong; tah; tay; song; sah; say; notr; noh; votr; voh; lerr; fahm; mah-ree; vol; o-rairr; sang-tür der say-kü-ree-tay; plahs; ah-tah-shay; prerm-yay; prerm-yairr.

Exercise 18

Translate:
1 Your first flight.
2 Fasten your seat belt.
3 Where are our tickets?
4 Here is her passport.
5 Here is his seat.
6 Their suitcases are in the plane.
7 Our timetable is important.
8 Where are my newspapers?

20 The expression c'est ('it is')

C'est facile.   It is easy.
C'est difficile.   It is difficult.
C'est très important.   It is very important.
C'est moins cher.   It is less expensive.

Vocabulary

possible	possible
impossible	impossible
magnifique	wonderful
affreux	dreadful

tôt	early
tard	late

IMITATED PRONUNCIATION: say; mwah*ng*; po-seebl; a*ng*-po-seebl;
mahn-yee-feek; ah-fre*r*; toh; tahr.

Exercise 19

Give the opposite of:
1 C'est intéressant.
2 C'est bon.
3 C'est possible.
4 C'est facile.
5 C'est magnifique.
6 C'est tard.

21 The time

If you intend to keep appointments, catch trains and buses etc., you
must be familiar with the way in which the French express the time:

Quelle heure est-il? What time is it?
Il est une heure. It is one o'clock.
Il est deux heures. It is two o'clock.
Il est trois heures. It is three o'clock.
Il est quatre heures. It is four o'clock.
Il est midi. It is midday.
Il est minuit. It is midnight.

Il est cinq heures et quart. It is a quarter past five.
Il est cinq heures et demie. It is half past five.
Il est six heures moins le quart. It is a quarter to six.

Il est six heures dix. It is ten past six.
Il est sept heures moins cinq. It is five to seven.

À quelle heure? At what time?
À huit heures. At eight o'clock.

À neuf heures du matin. At nine in the morning.
À neuf heures du soir. At nine in the evening.
À deux heures de l'après-midi. At two in the afternoon.

Vocabulary

le car	coach
le bateau	boat
l'aéroglisseur (*m.*)	hovercraft
le président	president, chairman
la conférence de presse	press conference
arriver	to arrive

Irregular verb:

partir (to leave)

Present tense
je pars
tu pars
il/elle part
nous partons
vous partez
ils/elles partent

IMITATED PRONUNCIATION (21): kel err ay teel; eel ay ün err; eel ay der zerr; trwah zerr; mee-dee; meen-wee; kahr; der-mee; ah kel err; ah ner verr dü mah-tang; dü swahr; der lah-pray-mee-dee; kahr; bah-toh; ah-ay-roh-glee-serr; pray-zee-dahng; kong-fay-rahngss der press; ah-ree-vay; pahr-teerr; pahr; pahr-tong; pahr-tay; pahrt.

Exercise 20

Add 15 minutes to the time stated:
1 Il est deux heures.
2 Il est quatre heures et quart.
3 Il est six heures moins le quart.
4 Il est huit heures cinq.
5 Le train arrive à dix heures.
6 Le car arrive à onze heures et demie.
7 Le bateau part à midi dix.
8 L'aéroglisseur part à minuit et demi★.
9 Le Président arrive à neuf heures.
10 La conférence de presse est à dix heures.

★Demi agrees with minuit (*m.*); write demie to agree with heure (*f.*).

22 Numerals

Here are some more numbers:

16	**seize**	33	**trente-trois**
17	**dix-sept**	40	**quarante**
18	**dix-huit**	41	**quarante et un**
19	**dix-neuf**	42	**quarante-deux**
20	**vingt**	50	**cinquante**
21	**vingt et un**	51	**cinquante et un**
22	**vingt-deux**	52	**cinquante-deux**
23	**vingt-trois**	60	**soixante**
30	**trente**	61	**soixante et un**
31	**trente et un**	62	**soixante-deux**
32	**trente-deux**		

IMITATED PRONUNCIATION (22): sez; dee-set; deez-weet; deez-nerf; va*ng*; va*ng*-tay-u*ng*; va*ng*t-der; va*ng*t-trwah; trah*ng*t; kah-rah*ng*t; sa*ng*-kah*ng*t; swah-sah*ng*t.

23 Seasons of the year

le printemps	Spring
l'été (*m.*)	Summer
l'automne (*m.*)	Autumn
l'hiver (*m.*)	Winter

The seasons are all masculine.

en été	in Summer
en automne	in Autumn
en hiver	in Winter
but	
au printemps	in Spring

24 Months of the year

janvier	January
février	February
mars	March
avril	April
mai	May

juin	June
juillet	July
août	August
septembre	September
octobre	October
novembre	November
décembre	December

Note that the months of the year are not written with a capital letter in French.

IMITATED PRONUNCIATION (23/24): le*r* pra*ng*-tah*ng*; lay-tay; loh-ton; lee-vairr; zhah*ng*v-yay; fayvr-yay; mahrss; ah-vreel; may; zhwa*ng*; zhwee-yay; oo OR oot; sep-tah*ng*br; ok-tobr; no-vah*ng*br; day-sah*ng*br.

25 Dates

Quelle date sommes-nous aujourd'hui?   What is the date today?
Nous sommes le deux janvier.   It's the 2nd January.
Nous sommes le huit février.   It's the 8th February.
Nous sommes le quinze mars.   It's the 15th March.
Nous sommes le vingt avril.   It's the 20th April.
Nous sommes le trente mai.   It's the 30th May.

Note: for the 'first' of each month we use **le premier**:

le premier juin	the 1st June
le premier juillet	the 1st July

but

le vingt et un août	the 21st August
le trente et un octobre etc.	the 31st October

Note also:

en août	in August
en septembre	in September
en octobre	in October
en novembre etc.	in November

Exercise 21

Write out in full the following dates:
1 New Year's Day
2 St. Valentine's Day
3 the first day of Spring
4 April Fools' Day
5 May Day
6 the Allied invasion of Normandy
7 the storming of the Bastille
8 the day French people begin their Summer holidays
9 the first day of Autumn
10 the Russian Revolution
11 Guy Fawkes Day
12 Christmas Day

26 Days of the week

lundi	Monday
mardi	Tuesday
mercredi	Wednesday
jeudi	Thursday
vendredi	Friday
samedi	Saturday
dimanche	Sunday

Note that the days of the week are not written with a capital letter in French.

Examples:
Avez-vous travaillé lundi?   Did you work on Monday?
Pierre téléphone jeudi.   Pierre is telephoning on Thursday.
Pierre téléphone le jeudi.   Pierre telephones on Thursdays.

Note: 'on' is omitted in French. **Le** indicates that the action takes place regularly.

IMITATED PRONUNCIATION (25/26): daht; oh-zhoor-dwee; lu*ng*-dee; mahr-dee; mairr-krer-dee; zher-dee; vah*ng*-drer-dee; sahm-dee; dee-mah*ng*sh.

Exercise 22

Translate:
1 I worked on Monday.
2 I listened to the radio on Tuesday.
3 I watched television on Wednesday.
4 I finished the report on Thursday.
5 I bought a record on Friday.
6 I telephoned my wife on Saturday.
7 I spoke Spanish on Sunday.
8 I work on Mondays.
9 She listens to the radio on Tuesdays.
10 We watch television on Wednesdays.

27 The position of adjectives

In French adjectives are usually placed after the noun:

un livre difficile	a difficult book
un médecin français	a French doctor
une voiture anglaise	an English car
une langue importante	an important language

The following adjectives normally precede the noun:

bon, bonne (*f.*)	good
mauvais	bad
petit	small
grand	large
joli	pretty
jeune	young
vieux (*m.sing. & pl.*)	old
vieil (*m.sing.* before a vowel or h)	
vieille (*f.*)	
vieilles (*f.pl.*)	
nouveau (*m.sing.*)	new
nouvel (*m.sing.* before a vowel or h)	
nouvelle (*f.*)	
nouveaux (*m.pl.*)	
nouvelles (*f.pl.*)	

Examples:

un bon employé	a good employee
un jeune pilote	a young pilot
un vieil ordinateur	an old computer
un nouvel électrophone	a new record player
une mauvaise cliente	a bad client
une jolie secrétaire	a pretty secretary

IMITATED PRONUNCIATION (27): zho-lee; zhern; vyer; vyay'ee; noo-voh; noo-vel; ahng-plwah-yay; klee-yahngt; ser-kray-tairr.

Vocabulary

Londres (*m.*)	London
l'argent (*m.*)	money
le départ	departure
la conversation	conversation
la semaine	week
les vacances (*f.*)	holidays
la nourriture	food
la chaleur	heat
l'intention (*f.*)	intention
la nage	swimming
visiter	to visit
trouver	to find
consulter	to consult
il faut	one must
indigeste	indigestible
insupportable	unbearable
moi	me (*see Lesson 8*)
un peu	a little
à l'avance	in advance
des	of the (**de** + **les** = **des**)

IMITATED PRONUNCIATION: longdr; ahr-zhahng; day-pahr; kong-vairr-sah-see-ong; ser-men; vah-kahngss; noo-ree-türr; shah-lerr; ang-tahng-see-ong; nahzh; vee-zee-tay; troo-vay; kong-sül-tay; eel foh; ang-dee-zhest; ang-sü-porr-tahbl; mwah; ung per; ah lah-vahngss; day.

CONVERSATION

À une agence de voyages à Londres.
Une conversation entre un employé français et une cliente anglaise. La cliente saisit l'occasion pour parler français.

Cliente Mon mari et moi, nous désirons passer deux semaines en France au printemps. Nous avons visité l'Italie en août, mais nous n'avons pas passé de bonnes vacances.

Employé Ah? Pourquoi pas?

Cliente Nous avons trouvé la nourriture un peu indigeste, nous avons trouvé la chaleur insupportable et nous avons dépensé beaucoup d'argent.

Employé Avez-vous l'intention de voyager en avion?

Cliente Non, en voiture, c'est moins cher.

Employé Un petit instant, Madame, je consulte l'horaire des aéroglisseurs. Il y a un départ à huit heures, à neuf heures, à dix heures, à onze heures, etc. Il faut réserver les places à l'avance.

Cliente Oui, oui, oui. Je n'ai pas l'intention de traverser la Manche à la nage!

TRANSLATION

At a travel agency in London.
A conversation between a French clerk and an English client. The client seizes the opportunity to speak French.

Client My husband and I wish to spend two weeks in France in the Spring. We visited Italy in August, but we didn't have a good holiday.

Clerk Oh? Why not?

Client We found the food a little indigestible, we found the heat unbearable and we spent a lot of money.

Clerk Do you intend to travel by plane?

Client No, by car, it's less expensive.

Clerk Just one moment, Madam. I'll consult the hovercraft timetable. There's a departure at eight o'clock, at nine o'clock, at ten o'clock, at eleven o'clock, etc. One must reserve seats in advance.

Client Yes, yes, yes. I don't intend to swim across (literally to cross at the swimming) the Channel!

Lesson 5

28 Regular verbs ending in -re

A number of important verbs end in **-re**:

vendre	to sell
rendre	to give back
attendre	to wait (for)
entendre	to hear
descendre	to take/bring down
répondre	to reply
perdre	to lose

We form the present tense by removing the **-re** from the infinitive and adding:

je	-s	**nous**	-ons
tu	-s	**vous**	-ez
il/elle	– –	**ils/elles**	-ent

je vends (I sell or I am selling)
tu vends
il/elle vend
nous vendons
vous vendez
ils/elles vendent

The perfect tense is formed by changing the **-re** of the infinitive into **-u**:

j'ai vendu (I sold or I have sold)
tu as vendu
il/elle a vendu
nous avons vendu
vous avez vendu
ils/elles ont vendu

Vocabulary

les parents (*m.*)	parents
le frère	brother
la musique	music
la maison	house
la mère	mother
cela	that
dépendre de	to depend on
défendre	to defend, to forbid

IMITATED PRONUNCIATION (28): vah*ng*dr; rah*ng*dr; ah-tah*ng*dr; ah*ng*-tah*ng*dr; day-sah*ng*dr; ray-po*ng*dr; pairrdr; vah*ng*; vah*ng*-do*ng*; vah*ng*-day; vah*ng*d; vah*ng*-dü; pah-rah*ng*; frairr; mü-zeek; may-zo*ng*; mairr; se*r*-lah; day-pah*ng*dr der; day-fah*ng*dr.

Exercise 23

Translate:
1 I am selling my car.
2 He is waiting for his wife.
3 We give back sixty francs.
4 That depends on my parents.
5 Do they (*f.*) hear the music?
6 She has sold her house.
7 We have not replied.
8 Have you brought down the luggage?
9 Are you (*fam. sing.*) waiting for your brother?
10 Have you (*fam. sing.*) lost your mother?

29 Irregular -re verbs

The following **-re** verbs are irregular, taking a slightly different pattern in the present tense and a very different pattern in the perfect tense.

prendre	to take
apprendre	to learn
comprendre	to understand
surprendre	to surprise

Present

je prends	I take (or I am taking)
tu prends	
il/elle prend	
nous prenons	
vous prenez	
ils/elles prennent	

Perfect

j'ai pris	I took (or I have taken)
j'ai appris	I learned
j'ai compris	I understood
j'ai surpris	I surprised

IMITATED PRONUNCIATION (29): prah*ng*dr; ah-prah*ng*dr; ko*ng*-prah*ng*dr; sür-prah*ng*dr; prah*ng*; prer-no*ng*; prer-nay; pren; pree; ah-pree; ko*ng*-pree; sür-pree.

Exercise 24

Change the present to the past and vice versa:
1 Est-ce que vous prenez le train?
2 J'apprends le français.
3 Avez-vous appris la langue?
4 Avez-vous compris?
5 Tu surprends souvent ton professeur?

30 Other irregular -re verbs

The following irregular **-re** verbs have a similar pattern to that of the 'prendre' group but the consonant is doubled in the nous, vous and ils/elles forms:

mettre	to put
permettre	to permit
promettre	to promise
soumettre	to submit

Present

je mets	I put (or I am putting)
tu mets	
il/elle met	
nous mettons	
vous mettez	
ils/elles mettent	

Perfect

vous avez mis	you put (or you have put)
vous avez permis	you permitted
vous avez promis	you have promised
vous avez soumis	you have submitted

Vocabulary

le matin	morning
le dictionnaire	dictionary
le projet	project, plan
l'enfant (*m.&f.*)	child
l'annonce (*f.*)	advertisement
la lettre	letter
permettre de	to allow to
promettre de	to promise to
rentrer	to return
tôt	early
tard	late
déjà	already

IMITATED PRONUNCIATION (30): metr; pairr-metr; pro-metr; soo-metr; may; met-*ong*; met-ay; met; mee; pairr-mee; pro-mee; soo-mee; mah-ta*ng*; deeks-yo-nairr; pro-zhay; ah*ng*-fah*ng*; ah-no*ng*s; letr; rah*ng*-tray; toh; tahr; day-zhah.

Note the construction with **défendre** and **permettre**:
Je défends à Paul de parler.   I forbid Paul to speak.
Je permets à Paul de parler.   I allow Paul to speak.

Exercise 25

Change the present to the past and vice versa:
1 Je mets une annonce dans le journal.
2 Il permet à sa secrétaire de partir tôt.
3 Vous promettez de répondre à la lettre?
4 Elle soumet le rapport ce matin.
5 Avez-vous mis le dictionnaire dans la valise?
6 Ont-ils permis à leurs enfants de rentrer tard?
7 Nous avons promis de parler français.
8 Avez-vous déjà soumis le projet?

31 Adverbs

We often need to describe *how* things are done, for example:

rapidly, admirably, carefully

In French, adverbs are formed by adding **-ment** to the adjective, which is the equivalent of **-ly** in English:

rapide becomes **rapidement** (rapidly)
admirable becomes **admirablement**
rare becomes **rarement**

If the adjective ends in a consonant, **-ment** is added to the feminine form:

immédiat   immédiate (*f.*)   **immédiatement**
général   générale (*f.*)   **généralement**
malheureux   malheureuse (*f.*)   **malheureusement** (unfortunately)

Vocabulary

attentif, attentive (*f.*)	careful
complet, complète (*f.*)	complete
lent	slow
normal	normal
principal	main
temporaire	temporary

IMITATED PRONUNCIATION (31): rah-peed; rah-peed-mah*ng*;
ahd-mee-rahbl; ahd-mee-rah-bler-mah*ng*; rahr; rahr-mah*ng*;
ee-mayd-yaht-mah*ng*; zhay-nay-rahl-mah*ng*; mah-ler-rerz-mah*ng*;
ah-tah*ng*-teef; ah-tah*ng*-teev; ko*ng*-play; ko*ng*-plet; lah*ng*; norr-mahl;
pra*ng*-see-pahl; tah*ng*-po-rairr.

Exercise 26

Form adverbs from the following adjectives:
1 rapide
2 facile
3 final
4 heureux
5 attentif
6 lent
7 complet
8 normal
9 principal
10 temporaire

32 The pronoun 'it'

When 'it' refers to something which has just been mentioned, we use
the same word in French as for 'he' or 'she', depending on the gender
of the noun:

Le vin? Il est très bon.   The wine? It's very good.
La voiture? Elle est chère.   The car? It's expensive.

Referring to things, 'they' is expressed by **ils** or **elles**:

Les trains? Ils sont rapides.   The trains? They're fast.
Les places? Elles sont réservées.   The seats? They're reserved.

Vocabulary

l'appareil (*m.*)	machine
le restaurant	restaurant
le produit	product
le message	message

le répondeur	telephone answering machine
automatique	
la poche	pocket
la qualité	quality
l'explication (*f.*)	explanation
clair	clear
en anglais	in English
excellent	excellent

IMITATED PRONUNCIATION: ah-pah-ray'ee; res-to-rah*ng*; pro-dwee; may-sahzh; ray-po*ng*-de*rr* oh-toh-mah-teek; posh; kah-lee-tay; eks-plee-kah-see-o*ng*; klairr; ah*ng* nah*ng*-glay; ek-sel-ah*ng*.

Exercise 27

Translate:
1 The report? It's very important.
2 The beer? It's bad.
3 The pocket? It's full.
4 The machine? It's excellent.
5 The restaurant? It's closed.
6 The quality? It's very good.
7 The products? They're French.
8 The messages? They're in English.
9 The explanation? It's not clear.
10 The answering machine? It's not expensive.

33 Personal pronouns – direct and indirect object

Study the following:

Michel le rencontre   Michel meets him
Michel la rencontre   Michel meets her
Michel les rencontre   Michel meets them
Hélène le vend (*masc. word*)   Hélène sells it
Hélène la vend (*fem. word*)   Hélène sells it
Paul nous félicite   Paul congratulates us
Paul vous félicite   Paul congratulates you
Sophie me choisit   Sophie chooses me
Sophie te choisit (*fam.sing.*)   Sophie chooses you
Sophie vous comprend (*fam.pl.*)   Sophie understands you

You will have noticed that:

a) 'me', 'him', 'her', 'us', 'them' etc. are placed *before* the verb in French

b) the words for 'him', 'her', 'it' and 'them' are just like the words for 'the'

c) the words for 'us' and 'you' are just like those for 'we' and 'you' (subject)

d) 'me' in French is **me**

e) 'you', familiar singular, is **te**

f) 'you', familiar plural, remains **vous**

Me, nous, vous and **te** can also mean '*to* me', '*to* us', '*to* you':

il me parle	he speaks to me
il nous répète	he repeats to us
elle vous répond	she replies to you
elle te vend (*fam.*)	she sells to you

Both '*to* him' and '*to* her' are translated by **lui**:

je lui répète	I repeat to him (or to her)

We express 'to them' by **leur**:

je leur parle	I speak to them

Sometimes the 'to' is not expressed in English, although clearly intended. Compare the French and the English below:

Je lui vends la voiture.	I sell him the car.
Nous leur téléphonons.	We telephone them.

Note: **me, le, la** and **te** become **m', l', t'** in front of a vowel or h:

il m'invite
elle l'écoute
je t'invite

Vocabulary

le client	client
le mode d'emploi	operating instructions
l'ami (*m.*)	friend
l'amie (*f.*)	friend
la leçon	lesson
la commerçante	shopkeeper
brancher	to plug in
mettre en marche	to start, to set going

IMITATED PRONUNCIATION: klee-yah*ng*; mod dah*ng*-plwah; ah-mee; ah-mee; ler-so*ng*; ko-mairr-sah*ng*t; brah*ng*-shay; metr ah*ng* mahrsh.

Exercise 28

Answer the questions using pronouns, as follows:

Vous me comprenez?   Do you understand me?
Oui, je vous comprends.   Yes, I understand you.

1 Elle me cherche?
2 Elle vous consulte?
3 Vous rencontrez le client?
4 Vous copiez la leçon?
5 Il invite Nicole?
6 Il exporte les voitures?
7 Comprenons-nous le mode d'emploi?
8 Branchons-nous la radio?
9 Mettons-nous l'appareil en marche?
10 Copions-nous le document?
11 Elles nous répondent en français?
12 Ils téléphonent à Pierre?
13 Ils téléphonent à Nicole?
14 Ils téléphonent à Pierre et à Nicole?
15 Vous parlez à la commerçante?
16 Vous répondez à vos amis?
17 Vous défendez à vos enfants de rentrer tard?

34 Direct object pronouns – agreement when used with perfect tense

When you use the direct* object pronouns with the perfect tense, there must be agreement, just as if you were dealing with an adjective:

je l'ai invité   I invited him
je l'ai invitée   I invited her
je les ai invités   I invited them (men or men and women)
je les ai invitées   I invited them (women)

vous l'avez copié   you copied it (le document)
vous l'avez copiée   you copied it (la leçon)
vous les avez copiés   you copied them (les documents)
vous les avez copiées   you copied them (les leçons)
vous les avez copiés   you copied them (les documents et les leçons)

il m'a trouvé   he found me (man speaking)
il m'a trouvée   he found me (woman speaking)
il nous a trouvés   he found us (men speaking)
il nous a trouvées   he found us (women speaking)
il nous a trouvés   he found us (men and women speaking)

elle vous a consulté   she consulted you (you, a male doctor)
elle vous a consultée   she consulted you (you, a female doctor)
elle vous a consultés   she consulted you (you, male doctors)
elle vous a consultées   she consulted you (you, female doctors)
elle vous a consultés   she consulted you (you, male and female doctors)

The pronunciation of all these endings is the same i.e. 'ay'. However, when the past participle ends in a consonant, for example **compris**, the addition of the feminine ending 'e' or 'es' results in this consonant being sounded:

je l'ai comprise   I understood her
                           zhe*r* lay ko*ng*-preez
je les ai apprises   I learnt them (les leçons, for example)
                           zhe*r* lay zay ah-preez

*NOT the indirect object pronouns i.e. 'to me', 'to him' etc.

Exercise 29

Answer the questions as follows:

Avez-vous rencontré le client?   Did you meet the client?
Oui, je l'ai rencontré.   Yes, I met him.

1 Avez-vous invité Pierre?
2 Avez-vous invité Nicole?
3 Avez-vous invité Pierre et Nicole?
4 A-t-il exporté les voitures?
5 A-t-elle consulté le médecin?
6 A-t-elle consulté la diététicienne?
7 A-t-elle consulté le médecin et la diététicienne?
8 Ont-ils branché la radio?
9 Ont-ils réservé les chambres?
10 Ont-ils perdu la clé?
11 Avons-nous compris le mode d'emploi?
12 Avons-nous compris la leçon?
13 Avons-nous compris les leçons?
14 Avons-nous compris les livres?
15 Avez-vous mis la cassette dans votre poche?

Vocabulary

l'appel téléphonique (*m.*)	telephone call
ici	here
tout	everything
même	even
depuis	since
peut-être	perhaps
il y a	ago
seul	single, only
utiliser	to use
aux (**à** + **les** = **aux**)	to the
répéter	to repeat

Note: **répéter** belongs to that group of verbs which undergo a slight change in spelling in the present tense (see section 81, lesson 12):

Present tense

je répète	**nous répétons**
tu répètes	**vous répétez**
il/elle répète	**ils/elles répètent**

---

lire (to read)

Present tense
je lis	nous lisons
tu lis	vous lisez
il/elle lit	ils/elles lisent

Perfect tense
j'ai lu, etc

---

faire (to do, to make)

Present tense
je fais	nous faisons
tu fais	vous faites
il/elle fait	ils/elles font

Perfect tense
j'ai fait, etc

être (to be)	**avoir** (to have)
Perfect tense	*Perfect tense*
j'ai été, etc	**j'ai eu**, etc

IMITATED PRONUNCIATION: ah-pel tay-lay-fo-neek; ee-see; too; mem; der-pwee; per-tetr; eel yah; serl; ü-tee-lee-zay; oh; ray-pay-tay; zher ray-pet; tü ray-pet; eel ray-pet; noo ray-pay-tong; voo ray-pay-tay; eel ray-pet; leerr; zher lee; tü lee; eel lee; noo lee-zong; voo lee-zay; eel leez; zhay lü; fairr; zher fay; tü fay; eel fay; noo fer-zong; voo fet; eel fong; zhay fay; etr; zhay ay-tay; ah-vwahr; zhay ü.

CONVERSATION

Une conversation entre une commerçante et un client.

Client Bonjour, Madame. Il y a deux semaines vous m'avez vendu un répondeur automatique.
Malheureusement, il ne répond pas aux appels téléphoniques de mes amis.

Commerçante Je suis surprise d'apprendre cela, Monsieur. Nos répondeurs sont d'excellente qualité. Avez-vous lu le mode d'emploi?

Client	Oui, je l'ai lu très attentivement. Attendez, je l'ai ici dans ma poche. Mais, où est-il? Je l'ai peut-être perdu.
Commerçante	Ce n'est pas grave, Monsieur. Avez-vous branché l'appareil correctement? Avez-vous mis l'appareil en marche? Avez-vous compris les explications?
Client	Oui, j'ai tout compris et j'ai tout fait correctement. J'ai même défendu à mes enfants de l'utiliser.
Commerçante	Permettez-moi de vous répéter, Monsieur, que nos produits sont d'excellente qualité. Si vous n'avez pas eu un seul message depuis deux semaines, la seule explication possible, c'est que personne ne vous téléphone!

TRANSLATION

A conversation between a shopkeeper and a customer.

Customer	Good morning. Two weeks ago you sold me an answering machine. Unfortunately, it doesn't answer my friends' telephone calls.
Shopkeeper	I'm surprised to hear (learn) that, Sir. Our answering machines are of excellent quality. Have you read the instruction booklet?
Customer	Yes, I read it very carefully. One moment (wait), I have it here in my pocket. But, where is it? Perhaps I've lost it.
Shopkeeper	It doesn't matter, Sir. Did you plug the machine in correctly? Did you start the machine? Did you understand the instructions (explanations)?
Customer	Yes, I understood everything and I did everything correctly. I have even forbidden my children to use it.
Shopkeeper	Allow me to repeat (to you), Sir, that our products are of excellent quality. If you haven't had a single message for two weeks, the only possible explanation is that no-one telephones you!

Lesson 6

35 Prepositions

Here are some useful French prepositions. Many of them are used to indicate position:

dans	in
en	in/to
sur	on
sous	under
devant	in front of
derrière	behind
près de	near
à côté de	next to
en face de	opposite
à	at/to
de	of/from
pour	for
avec	with
sans	without
après	after
avant	before

We saw in previous lessons that the French do not say '**à le**' or '**à les**' but **au** and **aux**; instead of '**de le**' and '**de les**', they say **du** and **des**.

Examples:

au musée	at/to the museum
à la boulangerie	at/to the baker's
aux magasins	at/to the shops
du bureau de poste	of/from the post office
de la pharmacie	of/from the chemist's
des hôtels	of/from the hotels
dans la voiture	in the car
en France	in/to France
à côté de la boucherie	next to the butcher's

en face de la poissonnerie	opposite the fishmonger's
près de l'épicerie	near the grocer's
sur la table	on the table
sous la chaise	under the chair
devant l'hôpital	in front of the hospital
derrière l'université	behind the university
avec mon mari	with my husband
sans difficulté	without difficulty
après le petit déjeuner	after breakfast
avant le dîner	before dinner

Note: Both **dans** and **en** mean 'in', but **dans** is more specific i.e. **dans** is generally used before **le, la, les, un, une, mon, votre** etc; otherwise **en** is used. Contrast:

dans la voiture de mon frère	in my brother's car
en voiture	by (in) car
dans le sud de l'Angleterre	in the South of England
en Angleterre	in England

Note also the following difference:

dans deux semaines   in two weeks' time
(I'll begin the work '**dans deux semaines**')

en deux semaines   within two weeks
(I did the work '**en deux semaines**')

36 The expression 'il y a'

We have already met **il y a**, but let us look at this very useful expression more closely. It means 'there is' or 'there are' and can, therefore, be used with both singular and plural nouns:

Il y a un taxi devant l'hôtel.   There's a taxi in front of the hotel.
Il y a des journaux ici.   There are some newspapers here.
Est-ce qu'il y a une banque ici?   Is there a bank here?

Vocabulary

le restaurant	restaurant
le supermarché	supermarket
le tunnel	tunnel

le numéro de téléphone	telephone number
le cinéma	cinema
le théâtre	theatre
le spectacle	show
l'ami (*m.*)	friend
les États-Unis	United States
la serviette	briefcase, towel, napkin
l'église (*f.*)	church
la librairie	bookshop
la bibliothèque	library
la cabine téléphonique	telephone booth
l'amie (*f.*)	friend
c'est difficile de	it is difficult to

Irregular verbs:

aller (to go)

Present tense
je vais
tu vas
il/elle va
nous allons
vous allez
ils/elles vont

venir (to come)

Present tense
je viens
tu viens
il/elle vient
nous venons
vous venez
ils/elles viennent

IMITATED PRONUNCIATION: We feel that you should now be fairly confident as far as the pronunciation is concerned and we are discontinuing the imitated pronunciation at this point. If you are still having difficulty with this aspect of the language, and it has to be admitted that French pronunciation does present problems, we strongly recommend that you purchase the cassette recordings which accompany this course.

Exercise 30

Translate:
1 There's a briefcase on the table.
2 There's a taxi in front of the hotel.
3 There's a restaurant behind the church.
4 There's a supermarket next to the bank.
5 There's a bookshop opposite the university.
6 Is there a telephone booth near the station?
7 Are there any English books in the library?
8 Is there a tunnel under the Channel?
9 I'm going to the cinema.
10 She's going to the United States.
11 Do you have the telephone number of the theatre?
12 I have bought a newspaper for my friend.
13 She's learning French with some cassettes.
14 It's difficult to work without my secretary.
15 Let's eat after the show.
16 Let's telephone before 9 o'clock.

37 Comparison of adjectives

In English we make comparisons by adding 'er' to the adjective or by using 'more' or 'less'; in French we simply put **plus** (more) and **moins** (less) in front of the adjective:

Cet hôtel est grand.   This hotel is large.
Cet hôtel est plus grand.   This hotel is larger.
Cette lettre est importante.   This letter is important.
Cette lettre est plus importante.   This letter is more important.
Ce livre est moins difficile.   This book is less difficult.

We express 'than' by **que**:

La cathédrale est plus belle que l'église.   The cathedral is more beautiful than the church.
Le film est moins intéressant que le livre.   The film is less interesting than the book.

Note also:

aussi . . . . . que   as . . . . as
pas si . . . . que   not so . . . as

L'aéroglisseur est aussi rapide que le tunnel sous la Manche.   The hovercraft is as fast as the Channel tunnel.
Le train n'est pas si rapide que l'avion.   The train is not as fast as the plane.

38 Comparison of adverbs

Adverbs follow the same pattern as adjectives:

Pierre travaille lentement.   Pierre works slowly.
Paul travaille plus lentement que Pierre.   Paul works more slowly than Pierre.

Vocabulary

le banquier	banker
le facteur	postman
le télégramme	telegram
le russe	Russian language
l'actrice	actress
courageux	brave
distinct	distinct
beau (*m.*)	beautiful
bel (*m.*) before a vowel or h	
beaux (*m.pl.*)	
belle (*f.*)	
belles (*f.pl.*)	

Exercise 31

Translate:
1 The banker is richer than the teacher.
2 The postman is poorer than the lawyer.
3 The air hostess is more beautiful than the actress.
4 The letter is less important than the telegram.
5 The pilot is as brave as the astronaut.
6 French is not so difficult as Russian (say *the* French . . . *the* Russian).
7 She speaks more distinctly than Paul.
8 He listens more attentively than his brother.

N.B. We have seen that 'than' is translated by **que**. However, when 'than' is followed by a number, we use **de** in place of **que**:

J'ai plus de 40 francs.   I have more than 40 francs.

39 Superlative of adjectives

In English, we form the superlative by adding 'est' to the adjective or by using 'most'; in French, we use **le plus**, **la plus** or **les plus**:

Pierre est le plus petit de la classe.   Pierre is the smallest in the class.
Annette est la plus grande de la famille.   Annette is the tallest in the family.
Pierre et Nicole sont les plus intelligents du groupe.   Pierre and Nicole are the most intelligent in the group.
Michel est le plus jeune pilote de la compagnie aérienne.   Michel is the youngest pilot in the airline company.

You will have noticed that 'in' is translated **de** after a superlative.

If the adjective is one that normally follows the noun, **le/la/les** are placed both before and after the noun:

le vin le plus cher   the dearest wine
les livres les plus intéressants   the most interesting books

40 Superlative of adverbs

We put **le plus** in front of the adverb, irrespective of the gender of the subject:

Annette travaille le plus rapidement de tous.   Annette works the fastest of all.

41 Irregular comparisons of adjectives and adverbs

bon (good) → **meilleur** (better) → **le meilleur** (the best)
bonne → **meilleure** → **la meilleure** (*f.*)

mauvais (bad) → **pire** (worse) → **le pire** (the worst)
Note that **plus mauvais** and **le plus mauvais** are also possible and, in fact, are more usual.

bien (well) → **mieux** (better) → **le mieux** (the best)
peu (little) → **moins** (less) → **le moins** (the least)
beaucoup (much) → **plus** (more) → **le plus** (the most)

Examples:

Un bon restaurant.	A good restaurant.
Un meilleur restaurant.	A better restaurant.
Le meilleur restaurant.	The best restaurant.
Je chante bien.	I sing well.
Vous chantez mieux.	You sing better.
Il chante le mieux de tous.	He sings the best of all.

Vocabulary

le parc	park
le monde	world
la ville	town
chic	smart
célèbre	famous
agréable	pleasant
confortable	comfortable
impressionnant	impressive

Exercise 32

You're showing a French friend around London. Try to convince him/her that 'British is best' by replying to your friend's comments like this:

Ce parc est grand.   This park is large.
Oui, c'est le plus grand parc du monde.   Yes, this is the largest park in the world.

1 Ce restaurant est chic.
2 Cette librairie est grande.
3 Ce magasin est célèbre.
4 Cette cathédrale est belle.
5 Cette bière est bonne.
6 Ce parc est agréable.
7 Londres est une ville intéressante.
8 La Rolls Royce est une voiture confortable.
9 Le Harrier est un avion impressionnant.

42 The weather

The French, like the British, often discuss the weather. The verb
faire appears in many expressions connected with this topic:

Il fait beau.   The weather is fine.
Il fait mauvais.   The weather is bad.
Il fait chaud.   It's hot.
Il fait froid.   It's cold.
Il fait du vent.   It's windy.
Il fait du soleil.   It's sunny.
Il fait du brouillard.   It's foggy.
Il pleut.   It's raining.
Il neige.   It's snowing.

Exercise 33

Which French expression describes the weather in the following
situations?

1 An umbrella would be useful.
2 Due to poor visibility, there could be some road accidents.
3 Hold on to your hat!
4 You'll need a warm overcoat.
5 Dark glasses would be a great help.
6 It's nice when this happens at Christmas.
7 Open the window and let in a little cool air.
8 Probably best to stay at home.
9 A walk through the park would be pleasant.

43 Verbs conjugated with 'être' (to be)

We saw in Lesson 4 that the past tense of most French verbs is formed
with **avoir** (to have):

j'ai téléphoné   I telephoned
vous avez fini   you finished

But some verbs, often denoting motion, form their past with **être**.
The following verbs, some of which are irregular, are the most
important:

aller (irreg.)	to go
arriver	to arrive
retourner	to return
monter	to go up
rester	to stay
partir (irreg.)	to leave
sortir (irreg.)	to go out
venir (irreg.)	to come
revenir (irreg.)	to come back
descendre	to go down

Note: when **monter** and **descendre** mean, respectively, 'to take up' and 'to bring down', they are conjugated with **avoir** (see Exercise 23).

Examples:

je suis allé	I went
je suis arrivé	I arrived
il est parti	he left
il est sorti	he went out
vous êtes venu	you came
vous êtes descendu	you went down

The past participle (**allé**, **parti**, **venu** etc.) of these verbs agrees in gender and number with the subject, just as if it were an adjective:

masc. sing.	*fem. sing.*
je suis allé	**je suis partie**
il est arrivé	**elle est sortie**
vous êtes retourné	**vous êtes venue**
tu es resté	**tu es descendue**

masc. pl.	*fem. pl.*
nous sommes allés	**nous sommes restées**
vous êtes partis	**vous êtes sorties**
ils sont revenus	**elles sont descendues**

Vocabulary

le bureau	office
l'étudiant (*m.*)	student
la réunion	meeting
la journée	day (daytime)
la maison	house, home

l'infirmière (*f.*)	nurse
l'étudiante (*f.*)	student
tout (*m.*)	all
tous (*m.pl.*)	
toute (*f.*)	
toutes (*f.pl.*)	

Exercise 34

A. Imagine for a moment the following:

You are a doctor (male). You arrived at the hospital this morning at 7 o'clock. You went to a meeting at 10 o'clock. You left the hospital with two nurses.

Now complete these sentences:
1 Je suis (doctor).
2 Ce matin je (arriver) à l'hôpital à 7 heures.
3 Je (aller) à une réunion à 10 heures.
4 Je (partir) avec deux infirmières.

B. Imagine the following:

You are a journalist (female). You went yesterday to a press conference. At one o'clock you went upstairs to the restaurant. You returned to the office very late.

Now complete these sentences:
1 Je suis (journalist).
2 Hier je (aller) à une conférence de presse.
3 Je (monter) au restaurant à une heure.
4 Je (retourner) au bureau très tard.

C. Consider the following:

Nicole and Sophie are students. They went to the university this morning at 9 o'clock. They stayed the whole day in the library. They came back home at 5 o'clock.

Now complete these sentences:
1 Nicole et Sophie sont (students).
2 Ce matin elles (aller) à l'université à 9 heures.
3 Elles (rester) toute la journée à la bibliothèque.
4 Elles (revenir) à la maison à 5 heures.

76

Vocabulary

l'ingénieur (*m.*)	engineer
hier	yesterday
déjà	already
tôt	early

Exercise 35

Translate:
1 The engineers arrived yesterday.
2 The actresses have already left.
3 We (*f.*) came back early.
4 You (*fam. sing. m.*) went downstairs.
5 Did the nurse stay all day?
6 Did you come back very late?

44 The expression 'je voudrais'

You will want to ask for things and to say what you would like to do; use **je voudrais** (I would like):

Je voudrais un café.   I would like a coffee.
Je voudrais de la confiture.   I would like some jam.
Je voudrais prendre le petit déjeuner dans ma chambre.   I would like to have (take) breakfast in my room.
Je voudrais rester deux jours.   I would like to stay two days.

Note: a) if you ask for **café**, you will receive black coffee; if you want white coffee, ask for **un café crème** or, at breakfast time, **un café au lait**.

b) **voudrais** is actually the conditional tense which we shall be studying later.

Vocabulary

le timbre	stamp
le plan	street map
le lait	milk
le sucre	sugar

le thé	tea
la carte postale	postcard
la note	bill (in a hotel)
l'addition (*f.*)	bill (in a restaurant)
régler	settle

Irregular verb:

envoyer (to send)

Present tense
j'envoie
tu envoies
il/elle envoie
nous envoyons
vous envoyez
ils/elles envoient

Exercise 36

Ask for the following, using je voudrais:
1 a postcard
2 a stamp
3 a street map of the town
4 an English newspaper
5 some milk
6 some sugar
7 some tea

And now, say that you would like:
8 to telephone London
9 to send a telegram
10 to settle the hotel bill

45 The expression 'il faut'

If you want to say that something has to be done, you can use **il faut** (one must, it is necessary):

Il faut conduire à droite. One has to drive on the right.
Il faut aller à la pharmacie. One has to go to the chemist's.

Used with the indirect object pronoun, **il faut** means 'need':

Il nous faut un dictionnaire.   We need a dictionary.
Il lui faut 50 francs.   He (or she) needs 50 francs.

Vocabulary

le crayon	pencil
le stylo-bille	ball-point pen
le papier à lettres	writing paper
la gomme	rubber
l'enveloppe (*f.*)	envelope
l'allumette (*f.*)	match

Exercise 37

Say you need the following:
1 a pencil
2 a ball-point pen

Now, she needs:
3 a rubber
4 some writing paper

Now, they need:
5 some envelopes
6 some cigarettes
7 some matches

Vocabulary

le port	port
le pain	bread
l'article (*m.*)	item
la place	square
la rue	street
la marque	brand
la promotion	special offer
la porte	door
l'année (*f.*)	year
tourner	to turn
recommander	to recommend

avoir le pied marin	to be a good sailor
tout droit	straight on
à gauche	on/to the left
à droite	on/to the right
d'habitude	usually
au revoir	goodbye
si	so
voilà	there is (pointing)
autre	other
rouge	red
quelques	a few
dernier, dernière (*f.*)	last

CONVERSATION

Un touriste anglais passe la journée à Boulogne.

Touriste   Pardon, Madame. Je cherche une bonne épicerie, ici près du port.

Passante   La meilleure épicerie de Boulogne est sur la place, en face de la banque. Vous allez tout droit et vous prenez la première rue à gauche.

Touriste   Merci, Madame. (*Il répète*) . . . je vais tout droit, je tourne à droite . . . non, non . . . je tourne à gauche. Ah, voilà l'épicerie.

À l'épicerie

Épicière   Bonjour, Monsieur. Vous désirez?

Touriste   Bonjour, Madame. Je voudrais du fromage, du vin et de la bière, s'il vous plaît.

Épicière   Voici le fromage. C'est la meilleure marque. Il est plus cher que les autres fromages, mais il est excellent. Je vous recommande aussi ce vin rouge. Il est moins cher que d'habitude; il est en promotion.

Touriste   Bien. Je prends ces trois articles. Merci. Est-ce que vous vendez aussi du pain?

Épicière   Non, Monsieur. Pour cela, il faut aller à la boulangerie. La boulangerie est à côté du bureau de poste.

Touriste   Merci. Au revoir, Madame. (*Il va à la porte*) . . . Oh, il pleut! Et il fait du vent.

Épicière   Attendez quelques instants. Ici à Boulogne il fait rarement beau. Il pleut souvent et il fait toujours du vent.

Touriste Oui. L'année dernière ma femme et moi, nous sommes venus passer la journée ici, mais il a fait si mauvais. Nous avons attendu . . . je n'ai pas le pied marin. Nous avons attendu un jour, deux jours. Finalement, nous sommes restés une semaine à Boulogne!

TRANSLATION

An English tourist spends the day in Boulogne.

Tourist Excuse me. I'm looking for a good grocer's, here near the port.

Passer-by The best grocer's in Boulogne is in (on) the square, opposite the bank. You go straight on and you take the first street on the left.

Tourist Thank you. (*He repeats*) . . . I go straight on, I turn to the right . . . no, no . . . I turn to the left. Ah, there's the grocer's.

At the grocer's

Grocer Good morning, Sir. What would you like? (lit. 'you wish?')

Tourist Good morning. I'd like some cheese, some wine and some beer, please.

Grocer Here's the cheese. It's the best brand. It's dearer than the other cheeses, but it's excellent. I also recommend (to you) this red wine. It's less expensive than usual; it's a special offer (lit. 'in promotion').

Tourist Fine. I'll take (lit. 'I take') these three items. Thank you. Do you sell bread?

Grocer No, Sir. For that one has to go to the baker's. The baker's is next to the post office.

Tourist Thank you. (*He goes to the door*) . . . Oh, it's raining. And it's windy.

Grocer Wait a few moments. Here in Boulogne the weather is rarely fine. It often rains and it's always windy.

Tourist Yes. Last year my wife and I came to spend the day here, but the weather was so bad. We waited . . . I'm not a good sailor (lit. 'I don't have the sea foot'). We waited one day, two days. Finally, we stayed a week in Boulogne!

Lesson 7

46 Adverbs of quantity

On occasions, you will need to talk about quantities; you may have too much of something or too little or not enough etc.

Study the following:

beaucoup	much, many
trop	too much, too many
tant	so much, so many
peu	little, few
assez	enough

When a noun follows these words, they are linked by **de** (**d'**):

beaucoup de temps (*m.*)	much time
beaucoup de légumes (*m.*)	many vegetables
trop d'argent	too much money
trop de vêtements (*m.*)	too many clothes
peu de patience (*f.*)	little patience
assez de fruits (*m.pl.*)	enough fruit

The following are also linked to the noun by **de** (**d'**):

plus	more
moins	less, fewer
autant	as much, as many

Examples:

J'ai l'intention de boire plus d'eau.   I intend to drink more water.
J'ai l'intention de manger moins de pain.   I intend to eat less bread.
Rémi a autant de disques que Marie-Claude.   Rémi has as many records as Marie-Claude.

Vocabulary

le mouchoir	handkerchief
le chapeau	hat
le pantalon	pair of trousers
le foulard	scarf
le cardigan	cardigan
le costume	suit
la chemise	shirt
la cravate	tie
la robe	dress
la jupe	skirt
la chemise de nuit	nightdress

Exercise 38

Answer the questions.

Example:

Vous faut-il une chemise?   Do you need a shirt?
Non, j'ai beaucoup de chemises.   No, I have many shirts.

1 Vous faut-il une cravate?
2 Vous faut-il un mouchoir?
3 Vous faut-il une robe?

Example:

Michel a acheté un chapeau?   Has Michel bought a hat?
Oui, il a maintenant trop de chapeaux.   Yes, he now has too many hats.

4 Bernard a acheté un pantalon?
5 Hélène a acheté une jupe?
6 Marie-José a acheté un foulard?

Translate:
7 He has little patience.
8 Have you put enough nightdresses in the suitcase?
9 I have more cardigans than Monique.
10 You have fewer suits than Pierre.

47 The future tense

You will often want to talk about what you plan to do in the future. There are three ways of doing this:

1 In conversation, you can often use the present tense with a future meaning:

Un petit instant, je finis ce rapport. One moment, I'll just finish this report. (See Lesson 3)
Bien. Je prends ces trois articles. Fine. I'll take these three items. (See Lesson 6)
J'arrive lundi. I'll arrive on Monday.

2 You can do what we do in English, i.e. use 'to go', followed by another verb:

Je vais téléphoner demain. I'm going to telephone tomorrow.
Aujourd'hui il va manger dans un restaurant chic. Today he's going to eat in a smart restaurant.
Nous allons regarder la télévision ce soir. We're going to watch television this evening.

3 You can use the future tense which is formed by adding the following endings to the infinitive of the verb:

je	– ai
tu	– as
il/elle	– a
nous	– ons
vous	– ez
ils/elles	– ont

Examples:

je consulterai	I will consult
tu chanteras	you (*fam.*) will sing
il fumera	he will smoke
elle exportera	she will export
nous choisirons	we will choose
vous finirez	you will finish
ils garantiront	they will guarantee
elles réussiront	they (*f.*) will succeed

To form the future of **-re** verbs, drop the final **e** of the infinitive before adding the endings:

j'attendrai	I will wait
il apprendra	he will learn
nous comprendrons	we will understand
vous mettrez	you will put
ils promettront	they will promise

Some important verbs have an irregular future and perhaps we should learn them now:

avoir	**j'aurai**	I will have
être	**je serai**	I will be
aller	**j'irai**	I will go
faire	**je ferai**	I will do, make
venir	**je viendrai**	I will come
envoyer	**j'enverrai**	I will send
il y a	**il y aura**	there will be
il faut	**il faudra**	it will be necessary

Vocabulary

le tennis	tennis
le week-end	weekend
le père	father
l'appartement (*m.*)	flat
la réunion	meeting
la conférence	conference
la mère	mother
les courses (*f.*)	shopping
international	international
étudier	to study
réparer	to repair
jouer	to play
visiter	to visit
tapisser	to wallpaper
organiser	to organise

Irregular verb:

écrire (to write)

Present tense
j'écris
tu écris
il/elle écrit
nous écrivons
vous écrivez
ils/elles écrivent

Perfect tense
j'ai écrit, etc

Exercise 39
Here is a list of things you plan to do tomorrow (*demain*). Translate the list into French, using the construction with *aller*. Write complete sentences.

1 Listen to radio
2 Buy newspaper
3 Study French
4 Do shopping

Here is Michel's list for next week (*la semaine prochaine*). Translate, using the future tense in complete sentences:

5 Repair car
6 Play tennis
7 Write letter
8 Visit museum

Here is Pierre and Hélène's list for next month (*le mois prochain*). Use the future tense, and write complete sentences:

9 Wallpaper flat
10 Organise meeting
11 Go to international conference
12 Spend weekend in London

Translate:
13 She will finish her letter.

14 We will go to the theatre next week.
15 You will surprise your father.
16 You (*fam.*) will choose your dress next month.

48 Modal verbs

These are auxiliary verbs which are used in conjunction with the infinitive of a following verb – for example, 'I can come' or 'We must telephone'. There are four important modal verbs in French:

pouvoir	to be able to
devoir	to have to
vouloir	to want to
savoir	to know (how to)

1. Sometimes you will want to talk about what you can or cannot do; use the irregular verb **pouvoir**:

Present tense: I can

je peux
tu peux
il/elle peut
nous pouvons
vous pouvez
ils/elles peuvent

Past tense (perfect): **j'ai pu**, I was able to

Future tense: **je pourrai**, I will be able to

Examples:

Je peux faire les courses maintenant.　I can do the shopping now.
Pouvez-vous me dire où est la gare?　Can you tell me where the station is?
Avez-vous pu téléphoner à Paris?　Have you been able to telephone Paris?

2. You will also want to talk about what you must or have to do; use the irregular verb **devoir**:

Present tense: I must

je dois
tu dois
il/elle doit
nous devons
vous devez
ils/elles doivent

Past tense (perfect): **j'ai dû,** I had to

Future tense: **je devrai,** I will have to

Examples:

Je dois changer ma vie.   I must change my life.
Vous devez envoyer une carte postale à votre ami.   You must send a postcard to your friend.
Il a dû partir.   He had to leave.
Elle devra apprendre l'espagnol.   She will have to learn Spanish.

3. We have already met the expression **je voudrais** meaning 'I would like'; this comes from the irregular verb **vouloir** (to want):

Present tense: I want

je veux
tu veux
il/elle veut
nous voulons
vous voulez
ils/elles veulent

Past tense (perfect): **j'ai voulu,** I wanted

Future tense: **je voudrai,** I will want

Examples:

Je veux changer mon argent anglais en francs.   I want to change my English money into francs.
Nous voulons une chambre pour deux personnes.   We want a double room.

A request can be made more polite by putting '**Voulez-vous** . . .' at the beginning of the sentence: **Voulez-vous signer ici?**   (Will you sign here?)

4. The irregular verb **savoir** means 'to know':

Present tense: I know

je sais
tu sais
il/elle sait
nous savons
vous savez
ils/elles savent

Past tense (perfect): **j'ai su,** I knew

Future tense: **je saurai,** I will know

Examples:

Je sais que vous voyagez à l'étranger.   I know that you travel abroad.
Savez-vous où je peux louer une voiture?   Do you know where I can hire a car?
Pierre saura demain s'il va être en chômage.   Pierre will know tomorrow if he's going to be unemployed (lit. 'in unemployment')

Savoir can also mean 'to know how to':

Je sais jouer du piano.   I can (know how to) play the piano.

Note the difference between **pouvoir** and **savoir**:

Je ne sais pas jouer du piano.   I can't play the piano. (I don't know how to)
Je ne peux pas jouer du piano.   I can't play the piano. (my hand is bandaged)

Vocabulary

le diplomate	diplomat
le marché	market
le contrat	contract
l'écriture (*f.*)	handwriting
arrêter	to stop

arrêter de fumer   to stop smoking
décourager   to discourage
nager   to swim
garer   to park
faire le tour   to tour the world
   du monde

Irregular verb:

conduire (to drive)

Present tense
je conduis
tu conduis
il/elle conduit
nous conduisons
vous conduisez
ils/elles conduisent

Perfect tense
j'ai conduit, etc

Exercise 40

Say that you can:
1 buy the vegetables at the market
2 prepare the report

Say that we cannot:
3 arrive on Monday
4 read his handwriting

Say that she must:
5 sign the contract
6 stop smoking

Say that they must not:
7 discourage the students
8 park the car in front of the hospital

Say that he wants to:
9 tour the world
10 spend less money

Ask your friend whether he/she knows how to:
11 drive
12 swim

49 Countries

In French, countries can be either masculine or feminine:

le Danemark	Denmark
le Portugal	Portugal
le Luxembourg	Luxemburg
le Canada	Canada
le Japon	Japan
le Pays de Galles	Wales
les États-Unis	United States
le Royaume-Uni	United Kingdom

la France	France
la Belgique	Belgium
la Grande-Bretagne	Great Britain
la Grèce	Greece
la Hollande	Holland
la Chine	China
la Russie	Russia
l'Angleterre	England
l'Écosse	Scotland
l'Allemagne	Germany
l'Italie	Italy
l'Espagne	Spain
l'Irlande	Ireland

Before a masculine country 'in' or 'to' is translated **au:**

au Pays de Galles	in/to Wales
au Portugal	in/to Portugal
au Japon	in/to Japan

Before a feminine country 'in' or 'to' is translated **en:**

en Angleterre	in/to England
en Écosse	in/to Scotland
en France	in/to France
en Chine	in/to China

We use **aux** for a country with a plural form:

aux États-Unis   in/to the United States

Exercise 41

Prepare a list of all twelve countries in the EEC and indicate whether they are masculine or feminine.

Exercise 42

Translate:
1 We spend our holidays in Greece.
2 Do you intend to go to Japan?
3 Great Britain exports cars to France.
4 Has the diplomat arrived in Russia?

50 Numerals

Let's continue our study of the numbers:

63	**soixante-trois**	81	**quatre-vingt-un**
70	**soixante-dix**	82	**quatre-vingt-deux**
71	**soixante et onze**	88	**quatre-vingt-huit**
72	**soixante-douze**	90	**quatre-vingt-dix**
73	**soixante-treize**	91	**quatre-vingt-onze**
79	**soixante-dix-neuf**	99	**quatre-vingt-dix-neuf**
80	**quatre-vingts**	100	**cent**

Note that the s in quatre-vingts is omitted when another number follows.

Exercise 43

Complete the following, writing the answers in words:

a $10 + 10 =$ g $40 + 30 =$
b $10 + 12 =$ h $19 + 60 =$
c $11 + 20 =$ i $40 + 41 =$
d $27 + 20 =$ j $41 + 50 =$
e $30 + 29 =$ k $19 + 80 =$
f $21 + 40 =$ l $50 + 50 =$

Vocabulary

la résolution	resolution
la liste	list
la promesse	promise
la gymnastique	physical exercises
la santé	health
certain	certain
neuf, neuve (*f.*)	brand-new
quoi	what
quoi de neuf?	what's new?
eh bien?	well?
vraiment	really
ça = cela	that
souhaiter	to wish
décider (de)	to decide (to)
excuser	to excuse

Irregular verbs:

boire (to drink)

Present tense
je bois
tu bois
il/elle boit
nous buvons
vous buvez
ils/elles boivent

Perfect tense
j'ai bu, etc

dire (to say, to tell)

Present tense
je dis
tu dis
il/elle dit
nous disons
vous dites
ils/elles disent

Perfect tense
j'ai dit, etc

CONVERSATION

Hélène prend des résolutions pour la nouvelle année.

Michel Bonjour, Hélène. Je suis venu vous souhaiter une bonne année.

Hélène Bonjour, Michel. Bonne année à vous aussi.

Michel Quoi de neuf?

Hélène Eh bien, j'ai décidé de changer ma vie. J'ai pris beaucoup de résolutions pour la nouvelle année.

Michel Vraiment? Et quelles sont ces résolutions?

Hélène Voici ma liste:

1 Je vais maigrir.

2 Je vais regarder la télévision moins souvent.

3 Je mangerai plus de légumes.

4 Je mangerai plus de fruits.

5 Je dépenserai moins d'argent en vêtements.

Mon mari m'a fait aussi quelques promesses. Voici sa liste:

1 Il va boire moins de bière.

2 Il va boire plus d'eau.

3 Il arrêtera de fumer.

4 Il fera de la gymnastique chaque matin.

5 Il rentrera plus tôt à la maison le soir.

Michel Et vous pensez que vous serez plus heureux?

Hélène Oui. Nous aurons plus de temps et plus d'argent. Nous serons tous les deux en meilleure santé.

Michel Et comment est-ce que vous dépenserez tout cet argent?

Hélène Nous achèterons une voiture neuve. Nous voyagerons à l'étranger plus souvent. Nous irons au Japon. Nous irons en Chine et aux États-Unis. Nous ferons le tour du monde.

Michel Excusez-moi, mais je dois dire que j'ai déjà entendu ça. Je l'ai entendu l'année dernière. Je ne veux pas vous décourager, mais je suis certain que vous ne ferez jamais rien!

TRANSLATION

Hélène makes (takes) some New Year resolutions.

Michel   Good morning, Hélène. I've come to wish you a happy New Year.

Hélène   Good morning, Michel. Happy New Year to you too.

Michel   What's new?

Hélène   Well, I've decided to change my life. I've made a lot of resolutions for the New Year.

Michel   Really? And what are these resolutions?

Hélène   Here's my list:

1 I'm going to slim.
2 I'm going to watch the television less often.
3 I'll eat more vegetables.
4 I'll eat more fruit.
5 I'll spend less money on (lit. 'in') clothes.

My husband has also made a few promises to me. Here's his list:

1 He's going to drink less beer.
2 He's going to drink more water.
3 He'll stop smoking.
4 He'll do exercises each morning.
5 He'll come home earlier in the evening.

Michel   Do you think that you will be happier?

Hélène   Yes. We'll have more time and more money. We'll both (lit. 'all the two') be in better health.

Michel   And how will you spend all this money?

Hélène   We'll buy a brand-new car. We'll travel abroad more often. We'll go to Japan. We'll go to China and to the United States. We'll tour the world (lit. 'We'll do the tour of the world').

Michel   I'm sorry (lit. 'Excuse me') but I must say that I've already heard that. I heard it last year. I don't want to discourage you, but I'm certain that you will never do anything! (Lit. 'that you will never do nothing').

Lesson 8

51 The imperfect tense

We have already seen that the perfect tense is used to talk about the past:

J'ai acheté un livre.

This sentence can be translated by 'I have bought a book', 'I did buy a book' or 'I bought a book'.

BUT sometimes you will want to say what you *used to do* at some specific time in your life. On these occasions you have to use the imperfect tense. To form this tense, take the **nous** form of the present tense, drop the **-ons** ending and add:

je	- ais	nous	- ions
tu	- ais	vous	- iez
il/elle	- ait	ils/elles	- aient

There is only one exception to the above rule, namely the verb **être**.

Examples:

je fumais	I used to smoke
tu chantais	you (*fam.*) used to sing
il organisait	he used to organise
elle choisissait	she used to choose
nous finissions	we used to finish
vous vendiez	you used to sell
ils lisaient	they used to read
elles écrivaient	they used to write

j'étais	I was
il était	he was
etc.	

j'avais	I had
il avait	he had
etc.	

We also use the imperfect tense when translating such sentences as 'I *was reading* the newspaper, when the telephone rang.' In other words, if the English construction is 'was/were . . . ing,' we require the imperfect tense in French.

Examples:

J'écoutais la radio, quand Michel a téléphoné.   I was listening to the radio, when Michel telephoned.
Elle prenait une douche, quand le facteur est arrivé.   She was taking a shower, when the postman arrived.

Vocabulary

le timbre	stamp
le bruit	noise
le porte-monnaie	purse
le cambrioleur	burglar
la traduction	translation
en haut	upstairs
en bas	downstairs
collectionner	to collect
jouer au football	to play football
aller à la pêche	to go fishing
faire de la photo(graphie)	to go in for photography
entrer dans la maison	to enter the house

Exercise 44

Here are some things that Bernard and Marie-Claude used to do, when they were younger; *translate using the imperfect tense:*
 1 He used to play football.
 2 He used to go fishing.
 3 He used to collect stamps.
 4 She used to sing.
 5 She used to listen to records.

We used to:
 6 learn Spanish
 7 live in a small house
 8 go in for photography

Translate:
9 I was finishing the translation, when I heard a noise upstairs.
10 She was doing the shopping, when she lost her purse.
11 They were watching television, when the burglar entered the house.

52 Relative pronouns

Study the following:

qui who, which, that (subject)
que whom, which, that (object)

Note: **que** becomes **qu'** in front of a vowel or h.

Examples:

L'automobiliste qui parle français. The motorist who speaks French.
La voiture qui est en panne (*f.*). The car which has broken down (lit. 'which is in breakdown').
L'auto-stoppeur que j'ai pris. The hitch-hiker whom I picked up.
Le camion que vous avez réparé. The lorry which you repaired.

If you're having difficulty in deciding whether 'who', 'which', 'that' is the subject or the object, here's a rule to help you:

if, in English, the verb comes immediately after 'who', 'which', 'that', use **qui**

if, in English, there is another word between 'who', 'which', 'that' and the verb, use **que**

Examples:

the car which has broken down **qui**
the car which I prefer   **que**

Note: in English, the relative pronoun is sometimes omitted, but it must always be expressed in French:

Le moteur que vous vérifiez. The engine you are checking.

You will remember that we learnt in Lesson 5 that the past participle (**invité, copié, trouvé**) has to reflect the gender and number of the direct object pronouns which are used with it; the same principle applies to the relative pronoun **que**:

Voici le permis de conduire que j'ai trouvé.   Here is the driving licence that I found.
Voici la carte que j'ai achetée.   Here's the map that I bought.
Voici les pneus que j'ai choisis.   Here are the tyres which I've chosen.

After a preposition 'whom' is also translated by **qui**:

Où est le mécanicien à qui vous avez téléphoné?   Where's the mechanic to whom you telephoned? (Where's the mechanic you telephoned?)

BUT 'which', after prepositions, is translated as follows:

lequel (*m.*)   **lesquels** (*m.pl.*)
laquelle (*f.*)   **lesquelles** (*f.pl.*)

The above words combine with **à** and **de** in the usual way:
auquel, duquel, desquels, desquelles.

Examples:

Le cric avec lequel il a changé la roue.   The jack with which he changed the wheel.
La galerie sur laquelle nous avons mis les valises.   The roof rack on which we put the suitcases.
Le garage auquel elle a envoyé son chèque.   The garage to which she sent her cheque.

In place of **de qui, duquel, de laquelle, desquels, desquelles**, the French often prefer to use the word **dont**:

L'autoroute dont nous parlons.   The motorway which we are speaking of (about).

We also use **dont** to mean 'whose':

L'automobiliste dont la femme est malade.   The motorist whose wife is ill.
Le garagiste dont je connais le frère.   The garage owner whose brother I know.

Note the unexpected word order in the last French sentence.

Sometimes 'which' in English refers not to a noun, as in our previous examples, but to a whole idea; in these cases use:

ce qui (subject)
ce que (object)

Examples:

Je ne peux pas lire ce qui est écrit ici.   I cannot read what is written here.
Je ne peux pas lire ce que Michel a écrit ici.   I cannot read what Michel has written here.

Vocabulary

le petit déjeuner	breakfast
le poste de télévision	television set
le vestibule	hall
le/la réceptionniste	receptionist
le fils	son
l'ascenseur (*m.*)	lift
la femme de chambre	chambermaid
la fille	daughter, girl
lourd	heavy
bilingue	bilingual
malade	ill
correct	correct
apporter	to bring
commander	to order
marcher	to walk, to work (machines)
donner sur	to overlook

Exercise 45

Translate:
1 The hotel, that you are looking for, is on the right.
2 I would like the room which overlooks the park.
3 The room, which we have reserved for you, is next to the lift.
4 I've brought the breakfast that your husband ordered.
5 Where's the television set which doesn't work?
6 The suitcases, which are in the hall, are very heavy.

7 The receptionist (*f.*), to whom you spoke, is bilingual.
8 The client, whose son is ill, is in room 5.
9 Didn't you understand what the chambermaid said to you?
10 The bill, that you have prepared, is correct.

53 The conditional tense

We use the conditional to say what we *would do*, (*if*) . . . This tense is formed by adding the following endings to the infinitive of the verb:

je	-ais	nous	-ions
tu	-ais	vous	-iez
il/elle	-ait	ils/elles	-aient

As with the future tense, if the infinitive ends in **-re**, omit the final **e** before adding the endings.

Examples:

je louerais	I would hire
tu inviterais	you (*fam.*) would invite
il habiterait	he would live
elle étudierait	she would study
nous choisirions	we would choose
vous finiriez	you would finish
ils comprendraient	they would understand
elles écriraient	they would write

When a verb is irregular in the future tense, it will have the same irregularity in the conditional tense:

j'aurais	I would have
tu serais	you (*fam.*) would be
il irait	he would go
elle ferait	she would do
nous enverrions	we would send
vous pourriez	you could, would be able
ils voudraient	they would like
elles sauraient	they would know
il faudrait	it would be necessary
il y aurait	there would be

The 'if' part of the sentence (i.e. 'if I had the time', 'if I spoke

French' etc.) is expressed in French by **si** (if), followed by the imperfect tense:

si j'avais le temps   if I had the time
s'il parlait français   if he spoke French
si vous vendiez votre maison   if you sold your house

Note: **si** becomes **s'** before **il** and **ils**.

The conditional is also used in French when the speaker or writer is repeating something he or she has heard but is unable to vouch for its accuracy. Compare:

Le père a donné son consentement au mariage.   The father has given his consent to the marriage.
Le père aurait donné son consentement au mariage.   Apparently, the father has given his consent to the marriage.

Vocabulary

le travail	work
l'interprète (*m.&f.*)	interpreter
l'enfant (*m.&f.*)	child
portugais	portuguese
marié	married
comme	as
dessiner	to draw

Irregular verb:

peindre (to paint)

Present tense
je peins
tu peins
il/elle peint
nous peignons
vous peignez
ils/elles peignent

Perfect tense
j'ai peint, etc

Exercise 46

Answer the questions as follows:

Qu'est-ce que vous feriez, si vous aviez beaucoup de temps?   What would you do, if you had a lot of time?
(write a book)
Si j'avais beaucoup de temps, j'écrirais un livre.   If I had a lot of time, I would write a book.

1 Qu'est-ce que vous feriez, si vous étiez riche?
   (tour the world)
2 Qu'est-ce que vous feriez, si vous ne travailliez pas?
   (paint and draw)
3 Qu'est-ce que Pierre ferait, s'il avait beaucoup de temps?
   (learn Portuguese)
4 Qu'est-ce que Nicole ferait, si elle parlait français?
   (work as an interpreter)
5 Qu'est-ce que Monique ferait, si elle parlait allemand?
   (work as a bilingual secretary)
6 Qu'est-ce que je ferais, si j'étais marié?
   (return home earlier in the evening)
7 Qu'est-ce qu'ils feraient, s'ils étaient en chômage?
   (look for work)
8 Qu'est-ce qu'elles feraient, si elles avaient des enfants?
   (stay at home)
9 Qu'est-ce que tu ferais, si tu avais le temps?
   (read a great deal)
10 Qu'est-ce que nous ferions, si nous voulions maigrir?
   (eat less and do exercises)

54 Disjunctive pronouns

We have already seen in Lesson 5 how the French express 'me', 'him', 'her', 'to us', 'to you' etc., when these pronouns are the object of a verb. But some of these pronouns have a different form when they:

1 follow a preposition
2 form part of a comparison
3 stand alone
4 follow the verb **être** (to be)

Thus:

moi	I, me	**nous**	we, us
toi	you (*fam.*)	**vous**	you
lui	he, him	**eux**	they, them (*m.*)
elle	she, her	**elles**	they, them (*f.*)

Examples:

Est-ce qu'il y a des lettres pour moi?   Are there any letters for me?
Je travaille en face de lui.   I work opposite him.
Nous sommes partis sans eux.   We left without them.
Il est plus petit que moi.   He's smaller than I.
Qui parle anglais ici? Elle.   Who speaks English here? She does.
C'est lui qui écrit toutes les lettres.   It's he who writes all the letters.

Vocabulary

le président	president
le programmeur	computer programmer
le poste de radio	radio set
le traité	treaty
la dactylo	typist
la femme de ménage	daily help
travailleur, travailleuse (*f.*)	hardworking
paresseux, paresseuse (*f.*)	lazy
casser	to break

Exercise 47

Replace the words in italics with a pronoun:

1 Je suis arrivé avec *Paul*.
2 Je voudrais avoir une place à côté de *la secrétaire*.
3 Nous avons l'intention de partir sans *Pierre et Monique*.
4 Anne est plus travailleuse que *les nouvelles dactylos*.
5 Michel est moins paresseux que *le nouveau programmeur*.
6 Qui a cassé mon poste de radio? *La femme de ménage*.
7 C'est *le président* et *le premier ministre* qui ont signé le traité hier.

55 The verbs 'savoir' and 'connaître'

In Lesson 7 we learnt that 'to know' is translated by **savoir**. This verb means to know a fact:

Savez-vous où est Paul?   Do you know where Paul is?
Je sais à quelle heure le train part.   I know at what time the train leaves.

BUT, when we talk about knowing a person or a place, that is to say when the meaning is 'to be acquainted with,' then we must use the irregular verb **connaître**:

Present tense

je connais	I know, I am acquainted with
tu connais	
il/elle connaît	
nous connaissons	
vous connaissez	
ils/elles connaissent	

Past tense (perfect): **j'ai connu,** I knew, I was acquainted with

Examples:

Je connais Paul, mais je ne sais pas où il habite.   I know Paul, but I don't know where he lives.
Vous connaissez Paris?   Do you know Paris?

Vocabulary

l'oncle	uncle
la tante	aunt
la machine à écrire	typewriter
libre	free
occupé	busy

Exercise 48

Translate:
1 I don't know if Paul has finished his work.
2 I don't know the Duponts.
3 Do you know where I can hire a typewriter?
4 Do you know if the doctor is free?
5 Does Marie-Claude know my aunt?

Exercise 49

In the CONVERSATION on the next page change all the familiar forms (tu, te, toi, ton) into the more formal vous/votre forms and make all necessary changes to the verbs.

Vocabulary

le cas	case, situation
les gens (*m.pl.*)	people
la visite	visit
la porte	door
la retraite	retirement
au-dessus de	above
chez	at someone's home or shop
bonsoir	good evening
justement	just
si	emphatic yes (used after a negative)
si	so
à propos	by the way
à mi-temps	part time
tout de suite	immediately
trop	too
inattendu	unexpected
bruyant	noisy
déranger	to disturb
arranger	to suit
frapper	to knock
penser à	to think of (thoughts)
penser de	to think of (opinion)
espérer	to hope

Note: **espérer** belongs to that group of verbs which undergo a slight change in spelling in the present tense (see section 81, lesson 12):

j'espère
tu espères
il/elle espère
nous espérons
vous espérez
ils/elles espèrent

CONVERSATION

Une visite inattendue

Pierre   Bonsoir Nicole, j'espère que je ne te dérange pas.

Nicole   Pierre! Bonsoir. Je pensais justement à toi.

Pierre   Tu n'es pas trop occupée?

Nicole   Non, non. J'écrivais une lettre, quand tu as frappé à la porte.

Pierre   Ah bon? À qui est-ce que tu écrivais?

Nicole   Aux Dupont.

Pierre   Les Dupont? Je ne les connais pas.

Nicole   Mais si! Les Dupont sont les gens qui habitaient au-dessus de chez nous à Paris, qui voyageaient beaucoup et dont les enfants étaient si bruyants.

Pierre   Ah oui. Je ne les connaissais pas très bien. À propos, comment va ton travail?

Nicole   Pas trop bien. Si seulement je pouvais travailler à mi-temps, ça m'arrangerait bien.

Pierre   Qu'est-ce que tu ferais de tout ce temps libre?

Nicole   Je peindrais, je dessinerais. Michel et moi, nous sortirions plus souvent, nous irions au cinéma, au restaurant. Je ferais du sport, j'apprendrais l'anglais, je lirais tous les livres que j'ai achetés l'année dernière, je . . .

Pierre   Tu ferais mieux de prendre ta retraite tout de suite!

TRANSLATION

An unexpected visit

Pierre   Good evening Nicole, I hope that I'm not disturbing you.

Nicole   Pierre! Good evening. I was just thinking of you.

Pierre   You're not too busy?

Nicole   No, no. I was writing a letter, when you knocked at the door.

Pierre   Really? (lit. 'oh good?'). Who were you writing to?

Nicole   To the Duponts (lit. 'To the Dupont').

Pierre   The Duponts? I don't know them.

Nicole   Yes, you do! The Duponts are the people who used to live above us (lit. 'above at our place') in Paris, who used to travel a great deal and whose children were so noisy.

Pierre   Oh yes. I didn't know them very well (lit. 'I used not to know them very well'). By the way, how's your work going?

Nicole   Not too well. If only I could work part time, that would suit me well.

Pierre   What would you do with (lit. 'of') all this free time?

Nicole   I would paint, I would draw. Michel and I (lit. 'Michel and I, we') would go out more often, we would go to the cinema, to the restaurant. I'd go in for sport (lit. 'I'd do some sport'), I'd learn English, I'd read all the books I bought last year, I . . .

Pierre   You would do well to retire immediately! (lit. 'You would do better to take your retirement immediately').

Lesson 9

56 Demonstrative pronouns

In English, a sentence like 'I prefer my doctor to the doctor who came this morning' would normally be shortened to 'I prefer my doctor to *the one* who came this morning'. In French, we express 'the one', 'those' as follows:

celui (*m.*)	the one
ceux (*m.pl.*)	those
celle (*f.*)	the one
celles (*f.pl.*)	those

Examples:

Je préfère mon médecin à celui qui est venu ce matin.   I prefer my doctor to the one who came this morning.
Cette infirmière et celle qui a pris votre tension.   This nurse and the one who took your blood pressure.
J'ai apporté vos comprimés et ceux de votre mari.   I've brought your tablets and your husband's (lit. 'those of your husband').

We would normally change 'this dentist and that dentist' to 'this dentist and *that one*'. In French, 'this one', 'that one', 'these', 'those' become:

masculine		*feminine*	
celui-ci	this one	**celle-ci**	this one
celui-là	that one	**celle-là**	that one
ceux-ci	these	**celles-ci**	these
ceux-là	those	**celles-là**	those

Examples:

Cet hôpital-ci ou celui-là?   This hospital or that one?
Quelle ambulance préférez-vous, celle-ci ou celle-là?   Which ambulance do you prefer, this one or that one?

Quels médicaments prenez-vous, ceux-ci ou ceux-là?   Which medicines do you take, these or those?

If you prefer not to refer to an object by name but to call it simply 'this' or 'that', you can use the following words:

ceci   this
cela (or **ça**)   that

Examples:

Je voudrais acheter ceci.   I'd like to buy this.
Le (or **la**) **malade m'a donné cela.**   The patient gave me that.

'This', 'that', 'these', 'those', followed by the verb 'to be', are all normally translated by **c'est** or **ce sont**:

C'est votre petit déjeuner, Monsieur.   This is your breakfast, Sir.
Ce sont (or **c'est**) **les ordonnances que vous avez demandées.** These are the prescriptions you asked for.

C'est, ce sont can also mean 'he/she is' and 'they are':

C'est un dentiste (or **Il est dentiste**).   He's a dentist.

Vocabulary

le rhume	cold
le coeur	heart
le prince	prince
le chirurgien	surgeon
le/la kinésithérapeute	physiotherapist
le pharmacien	chemist
le rendez-vous	appointment
la greffe	transplant
la soeur	sister
la princesse	princess
la pharmacienne	chemist
moderne	modern
effectuer	to carry out

Exercise 50

Translate:

1 My cold is worse than my sister's.
2 This hospital is more modern than the one the Princess visited last year.
3 Which surgeon carried out the heart transplant? This one or that one?
4 Have you an appointment with this dentist or that one?
5 The physiotherapist gave me this.
6 The chemist prepared that.
7 This is your new secretary.
8 These are your patients.

57 Possessive pronouns

Instead of saying 'The waiter has brought your soup but not my soup', we would usually say 'The waiter has brought your soup but not *mine*'. In French, possessive pronouns ('mine', 'yours', 'hers' etc.) must agree with the noun they replace and are expressed as follows:

Pronouns replacing masc. nouns

sing.	*plural*	
le mien	**les miens**	mine
le tien	**les tiens**	yours (*fam.*)
le sien	**les siens**	his/hers
le nôtre	**les nôtres**	ours
le vôtre	**les vôtres**	yours
le leur	**les leurs**	theirs

Pronouns replacing fem. nouns

sing.	*plural*	
la mienne	**les miennes**	mine
la tienne	**les tiennes**	yours (*fam.*)
la sienne	**les siennes**	his/hers
la nôtre	**les nôtres**	ours
la vôtre	**les vôtres**	yours
la leur	**les leurs**	theirs

Examples:

Le garçon a apporté votre soupe, mais pas la mienne.   The waiter has brought your soup, but not mine.

Voici son croissant, mais où est le vôtre?   Here's his/her croissant, but where's yours?

Notre jambon est très bon; comment est le leur?   Our ham is very good; how's theirs?

Ma bière est excellente; est-ce que la vôtre est bonne aussi?   My beer is excellent; is yours good too?

J'ai payé mon café, mais je n'ai pas payé les leurs.   I've paid for my coffee, but I haven't paid for theirs.

When following the verb 'to be' and having the meaning of 'belonging to', the possessive pronouns are often translated by:

à moi	à nous
à toi	à vous
à lui	à eux (*m.pl.*)
à elle	à elles (*f.pl.*)

It is also possible to say **à Pierre, à ma femme** etc., meaning Pierre's, my wife's:

Pardon, Madame, est-ce que ce parapluie est à vous?   Excuse me, Madam, is this umbrella yours?

Ces gants (*m.*) ne sont pas à moi; ils sont à mon frère.   These gloves are not mine; they belong to my brother.

58 More interrogatives

WHAT . . .? is expressed as follows:

a) after a preposition – **quoi**

À quoi pensez-vous?   What are you thinking about?
Je pense à mon déjeuner.   I'm thinking about my lunch.
Avec quoi avez-vous payé le dîner?   What did you pay for the dinner with?
J'ai payé avec ma carte de crédit.   I paid with my credit card.

b) after the verb 'to be' and a noun – **quel, quelle, quels, quelles**

Quel est votre nom?   What is your name?
Quel est votre numéro de téléphone?   What is your telephone number?
Quelle est votre adresse?   What is your address?
Quels sont les prix?   What are the prices?

c) when subject of the sentence – **qu'est-ce qui**

Délicieux? Qu'est-ce qui est délicieux?   Delicious? What's delicious?

d) When object of the sentence – **qu'est-ce que** or **que (qu')**

Qu'est-ce que vous avez comme légumes?   What have you got in the way of vegetables?
or
Qu'avez-vous comme légumes?

e) As an exclamation 'What!' is translated **Quoi!**

Quoi! Le service n'est pas compris?   What! The service isn't included?
Quoi! Le bar est fermé?   What! The bar is closed?
Quoi! Le café n'est pas ouvert?   What! The cafe isn't open?

f) As an exclamation, 'what' followed by a noun is translated by **quel, quelle, quels, quelles**:

Quel repas!   What a meal!
Quelle cuisinière!   What a cook!

WHO, WHOM . . .? is expressed as follows: (see also Lesson 3)

a) when subject of the sentence – **qui** or **qui est-ce qui**

Qui est-ce qui a réservé la table?   Who reserved the table?

b) when object of the sentence – **qui** or **qui est-ce que**

Qui est-ce que vous avez payé? La serveuse?   Whom did you pay? The waitress?

c) **Avec qui avez-vous mangé?**   Who(m) did you eat with?

WHICH ONE(S) . . .? is expressed by – **lequel, laquelle, lesquels, lesquelles:**

Voici trois bons vins. À votre avis, lequel est le meilleur? Here are three good wines. In your opinion, which one is the best?
Toutes les tables sont libres, Madame; laquelle préférez-vous? All the tables are free, Madam; which one do you prefer?
Des légumes? Oui, lesquels voulez-vous? Vegetables? Yes, which would you like?

We saw in Lesson 3 that 'Which book?', 'Which house?' etc. are translated **Quel livre? Quelle maison?** For example:

À quel restaurant avez-vous l'intention d'aller? Which restaurant do you intend to go to?

But remember that in French the past participle of a verb conjugated with avoir takes the same gender and number as the direct object, when this direct object precedes the past participle (see also Lesson 5):

Quel vin avez-vous bu? Which wine did you drink?
Quelle viande avez-vous mangée? Which meat did you eat?
Quels plats avez-vous recommandés? Which dishes did you recommend?
Quelles pommes avez-vous achetées? Which apples did you buy?

WHOSE . . .? is translated by **à qui:**

À qui est ce dessert? Whose is this dessert?
À qui est cette serviette? Whose is this napkin?

Vocabulary

le barman	barman
le whisky	whisky
le poisson	fish
le repas	meal
le couteau	knife
le chapeau	hat
la fourchette	fork
la cuillère	spoon

les baguettes (*f.*)	chopsticks
frais, fraîche (*f.*)	fresh
chinois	Chinese
italien	Italian
commander	to order

Irregular verbs:

sentir (to smell)

je sens
tu sens
il/elle sent
nous sentons
vous sentez
ils/elles sentent

partir (to leave)

je pars
tu pars
il/elle part
nous partons
vous partez
ils/elles partent

servir (to serve)

je sers
tu sers
il/elle sert
nous servons
vous servez
ils/elles servent

Note: **payer** (to pay) is not irregular, but is one of those verbs which changes its spelling in the stem (see section 81). As seen in the following present tense, **y** becomes **i** before a silent **e**.

je paie	**nous payons**
tu paies	**vous payez**
il/elle paie	**ils/elles paient**

Exercise 51

Translate:

1 The barman has served you your whisky, but where's mine?
2 My fish is delicious; yours is not fresh.
3 I've paid our bill and they've paid theirs.
4 Does this hat belong to you or to your friend (*m.*)?
5 What do you want to eat this Chinese meal with? With chopsticks?
 What! No! With a knife and fork.
6 What is the telephone number of the Italian restaurant?
7 Which vegetables did she order?
8 What smells so good?
9 Here's a list of the best restaurants in Paris; which one do you
 prefer?
10 Whose is this spoon?

59 More adverbs

We can form adverbs from adjectives ending in **-ant**, **-ent** by changing
the **-nt** to **-mment**:

constant becomes **constamment**   constantly
évident becomes **évidemment**   obviously

Note: an important exception is **lent, lentement** 'slowly'.

A few adjectives can be used as adverbs without any change:

La soupe sent bon.   The soup smells good.
Le poisson sent mauvais.   The fish smells bad.
Frappez fort.   Knock loudly.
Parlez plus bas.   Speak more softly.

Here is a list of useful adverbs and adverbial expressions (see also
Lesson 5):

Time
tôt   early
tard   late
maintenant   now
tout de suite immediately
immédiatement immediately

ensuite	afterwards
toujours	always, still
hier	yesterday
aujourd'hui	today
demain	tomorrow
ce matin	this morning
cet après-midi	this afternoon
ce soir	this evening
souvent	often
rarement	rarely

Place

ici	here
là	here, there
là-bas	over there
à droite	on/to the right
à gauche	on/to the left
en haut	upstairs
en bas	downstairs
partout	everywhere

Certainty

sûrement	certainly, surely
certainement	certainly

Doubt

peut-être	perhaps
probablement	probably

Manner

bien	well
mal	badly
ensemble	together
surtout	especially
exprès	on purpose
vite	quickly
rapidement	rapidly
lentement	slowly
déjà	already
encore	still, yet

60 Position of adverbs

In French, adverbs are placed after the verb, never between the subject and verb, as in English:

Il parle rarement anglais.   He rarely speaks English.
Elle va souvent au théâtre.   She often goes to the theatre.

In compound tenses (e.g. the perfect tense) the following adverbs are normally placed between **avoir** (or **être**) and the past participle:

bien	**toujours**
mal	**souvent**
vite	**beaucoup**
encore	**déjà**

Examples:

Vous avez bien répondu à la question.   You have answered the question well.
Je n'ai pas encore lu votre lettre.   I haven't read your letter yet.
Votre frère est déjà parti?   Has your brother already left?

But when the adverb is an important word in the sentence, it generally comes at the end:

Je vais écrire la lettre maintenant.   I'm going to write the letter now.

Vocabulary

le bain	bath
neiger	to snow
pleuvoir	to rain
taper à la machine	to type

Exercise 52

Give the opposite of:
1 Elle tape vite à la machine.
2 Ils chantent bien.
3 Ne parlez pas si fort.
4 Il va rarement chez ses parents.
5 Nous n'avons pas encore mangé.

6 Il va peut-être pleuvoir ou neiger.
7 Elle prend un bain en haut.
8 Elles feront les courses demain.

Vocabulary

le mariage	wedding, marriage
le mannequin	model, dummy
la veste	jacket
la taille	size
la couleur	colour
la mode	fashion
la laine	wool
la vitrine	shop window
la vente	sale
bleu marine	navy blue
gris clair	light grey
pur	pure
court	short
long, longue (*f.*)	long
heureusement	fortunately
malheureusement	unfortunately
exactement	exactly
le dernier cri	the latest fashion
être en train de	to be in the middle of (doing something)
essayer	to try, to try on
ne . . (verb) . . que	only

Irregular verb:

plaire (to please)

Present tense

je plais
tu plais
il/elle plaît
nous plaisons
vous plaisez
ils/elles plaisent

Perfect tense
j'ai plu, etc

CONVERSATION

Une veste dernier cri

Client	Bonjour, Madame. Je vais à un mariage la semaine prochaine . . . heureusement pas le mien . . . et je voudrais acheter une veste . . . une veste très chic . . . une veste dernier cri.
Vendeuse	Oui, quelle est votre taille, Monsieur?
Client	En Angleterre je fais du 42.
Vendeuse	Quelle couleur préférez-vous?
Client	Je veux surtout une couleur à la mode.
Vendeuse	Eh bien, j'ai cette veste-ci en bleu marine en pure laine, et celle-là en gris clair.
Client	Hm, j'aurais préféré une veste comme celle que vous avez en vitrine. Elle me plaît beaucoup.
Vendeuse	Malheureusement, je n'ai plus votre taille, Monsieur. Je n'ai que des petites tailles.
Client	Et celle sur le mannequin, ici dans le magasin?
Vendeuse	C'est aussi une petite taille. Je pense qu'elle sera trop courte pour vous.
Client	Mais . . . regardez! Regardez celle-là! C'est exactement ce qu'il me faut. Je vais l'essayer tout de suite.
Vendeuse	Non, non, non, Monsieur! Cette veste-là n'est pas en vente. Elle est à ce monsieur là-bas qui est en train d'essayer un costume!

TRANSLATION

The latest thing in jackets (lit. 'A jacket latest cry')

Customer	Good morning. I'm going to a wedding next week . . . fortunately not mine . . . and I'd like to buy a jacket . . . a very smart jacket . . . the latest thing in jackets.
Saleslady	Yes, What is your size, Sir?
Customer	In England I take size 42 (lit. 'I do some 42').
Saleslady	What colour do you prefer?
Customer	I particularly want a colour that's in fashion.
Saleslady	Well, I have this jacket in navy blue in pure wool, and that one in light grey.
Customer	Hm, I would have preferred a jacket like the one you have

in the window. I like it very much (lit. 'It pleases me
much').

Saleslady   Unfortunately, I no longer have your size, Sir. I have only
small sizes.

Customer   What about (lit. 'And') the one which is on the model,
here in the shop?

Saleslady   That's also a small size. I think it will be too short for you.

Customer   But . . . look! Look at that one! That's exactly what I
need. I'm going to try it on right away.

Saleslady   No, no, no, Sir, that jacket is not for sale! It belongs to
that gentleman over there who's trying on a suit!

Lesson 10

61 Reflexive verbs

Study the following:

laver	to wash	**se laver**	to wash oneself
raser	to shave	**se raser**	to shave oneself
brûler	to burn	**se brûler**	to burn oneself
perdre	to lose	**se perdre**	to lose oneself
couper	to cut	**se couper**	to cut oneself
préparer	to prepare	**se préparer**	to prepare oneself
amuser	to amuse	**s'amuser**	to enjoy oneself
habiller	to dress	**s'habiller**	to dress oneself

The verbs in the second column are being used reflexively and are conjugated as follows:

Present tense

je me lave	I wash myself
tu te rases	you (*fam.*) shave yourself
il se brûle	he burns himself
elle se prépare	she prepares herself
nous nous amusons	we enjoy ourselves
vous vous habillez	you dress yourself (yourselves)
ils se perdent	they (*m.*) lose themselves
elles se coupent	they (*f.*) cut themselves

Note: **me, te** and **se** become **m', t'** and **s'** before a vowel or h.

All reflexive verbs form their compound tenses with **être**. The past participle agrees in gender and number with the preceding direct object.

Perfect tense

je me suis lavé(e)	I washed myself
tu t'es habillé(e)	you (*fam.*) dressed yourself
il s'est rasé	he shaved himself
elle ne s'est pas amusée	she did not enjoy herself

nous nous sommes préparé(e)s	we prepared ourselves
vous ne vous êtes pas perdu(e)	you didn't lose yourself
vous ne vous êtes pas perdu(e)s	you didn't lose yourselves
ils se sont brûlés	they burnt themselves
elles ne se sont pas coupées	they didn't cut themselves

Imperfect tense
je me lavais   I used to wash or I was washing myself

Future tense
je me laverai   I will wash myself

Conditional tense
je me laverais   I would wash myself

Note that in English we don't always add the reflexive pronoun, but say simply 'I wash', 'he shaves'. In French the reflexive pronoun must always be expressed. Compare:

Je me rase.   I shave.
Je rase mon père.   I shave my father.

Reflexive verbs are much more common in French than in English. Here is a list for reference:

se déshabiller	to undress oneself
s'endormir	to fall asleep
se réveiller	to wake up
se lever	to get up
se dépêcher	to hurry
se promener	to go for a walk
se reposer	to rest
se coucher	to go to bed
se tromper	to make a mistake
s'appeler	to be called
se marier	to get married
se débarrasser de	to get rid of
se servir de	to make use of
se souvenir de	to remember

It is important to distinguish between reflexive pronouns and pronouns which are merely used for emphasis. Compare:

Je lave les enfants.   I wash the children.
Je me lave.   I wash myself.
Je lave les enfants moi-même.   I wash the children myself.

These emphatic pronouns are:

moi-même   **nous-mêmes**
toi-même   **vous-même(s)**
lui-même   **eux-mêmes**
elle-même   **elles-mêmes**

Vocabulary

se peigner   to comb one's hair
se maquiller   to put on one's make-up
se laver les mains (*f.*)   to wash one's hands
se brosser les dents (*f.*) to brush one's teeth

Exercise 53

This is what Paul does each day.

Translate:
1 He wakes up at 7 a.m.
2 He washes.
3 He shaves.
4 He goes to work.

And now Monique:
5 She gets up at 8 a.m.
6 She takes a shower.
7 She combs her hair.
8 She puts her make-up on.
9 She goes to the station.

This is what you and I do:
10 We wash.
11 We dress quickly.
12 We go for a walk.
13 We go to bed at 10 p.m.

Translate:
14 I (*f.*) have enjoyed myself.
15 You (*f.*) have not made a mistake.
16 They (*f.*) are resting.
17 They (*m.*) have washed the car themselves.
18 We brush our teeth each morning.

Reflexive pronouns are also used in sentences where we use the expression 'each other':

Nous nous sommes souvent rencontrés.   We often met.
Le président américain et le dirigeant soviétique ne se comprennent pas.   The American President and the Soviet Leader do not understand each other.

Note that the past participle of reflexive verbs does not agree with a preceding *indirect* object (i.e. when the meaning is *to* or *for* myself, himself etc.). Compare:

Ils se sont rencontrés.   They met each other.
Ils se sont téléphoné.   They telephoned (to) each other.

62 Verbs preceded by prepositions

Study the following:

a) I'm used *to getting up* very early.
b) He left *without saying* goodbye.
c) She hesitated *before replying*.
d) *After buying* a computer, he worked much more quickly.
e) These cassettes are excellent *for improving* one's pronunciation.
f) He began *by criticising* the managing director.

You will have noticed that, in English, verbs preceded by a preposition end in -ing. In French, the infinitive is used:

a) **Je suis habitué à me lever très tôt.**
b) **Il est parti sans dire au revoir.**
c) **Elle a hésité avant de répondre.**
d) **Après avoir acheté un ordinateur, il a travaillé beaucoup plus vite.**
e) **Ces cassettes sont excellentes pour améliorer sa prononciation.**
f) **Il a commencé par critiquer le président-directeur général.**

There is one exception to the above rule, namely the preposition **en**, which is followed by the present participle. This will be dealt with in the next lesson.

Note also that, although the English is usually 'after buying' etc., the French has to be 'after having bought', **après avoir acheté** or, in the case of those verbs conjugated with **être**, **après être** . . .

Vocabulary

le mot	word
le ménage	housework
le poste de radio	radio set
l'électricien (*m.*)	electrician
la lampe	lamp
l'émission (*f.*)	broadcast
partir	to leave
quitter	to leave (with object)
capter	to pick up (broadcast)
tout le monde	everyone

Exercise 54

Translate:
1 He left the house without saying a word.
2 She's used to listening to records in her bedroom.
3 Before repairing the lamp, he telephoned the electrician.
4 After preparing breakfast, she did the housework.
5 My mother began by saying that the family was in good health and finished by wishing everyone a happy New Year.
6 This radio set is excellent for picking up French broadcasts.

63 Translation of 'to' before an infinitive

Compare the following French and English sentences:

a) **Je dois apprendre le français.**   I must learn French.
b) **J'ai décidé d'apprendre le français.**   I have decided to learn French.
c) **J'ai commencé à apprendre le français.**   I have started to learn French.
d) **J'ai acheté ce livre pour apprendre le français.**   I have bought this book to learn French.

You will see from the above sentences that 'to' coming before an infinitive is sometimes:

a) not translated
b) translated by **de (d')**

c) translated by **à**
d) translated by **pour**

Unfortunately, there is only one rule to help us decide which preposition to use and it's this:
when 'to' means 'in order to', use **pour**.

The rest of the time it's simply a question of learning by heart which verbs take *no* preposition, which take **de** and which take **à**.

Here are some lists for reference (see Hugo's 'French Verbs Simplified' for complete lists).

'To' is not translated before an infinitive coming after these verbs:

aimer	to like, to love
préférer	to prefer
vouloir	to want
désirer	to wish
aller	to go
venir	to come
devoir	to have to
falloir (il faut)	to be necessary
espérer	to hope
pouvoir	to be able
savoir	to know how

'To' is translated by **de** before an infinitive coming after these verbs:

cesser	to stop
conseiller	to advise
décider	to decide
demander	to ask
dire	to tell
empêcher	to prevent
essayer	to try
éviter	to avoid
finir	to finish
oublier	to forget
permettre	to allow
persuader	to persuade
promettre	to promise
proposer	to propose
refuser	to refuse
regretter	to regret

Note also:

être content de	to be pleased to
être heureux de	to be happy to
être ravi de	to be delighted to
être triste de	to be sad to
être désolé de	to be sorry to
avoir l'intention de	to intend to
avoir l'occasion de	to have the opportunity to
avoir le temps de	to have the time to
avoir le plaisir de	to have the pleasure to
il est facile de	it is easy to
il est difficile de	it is difficult to
il est possible de	it is possible to
il est impossible de	it is impossible to
il est permis de	it is permitted to
il est défendu de	it is forbidden to
il est temps de	it is time to

'To' is translated by à before an infinitive coming after these verbs:

aider	to help
apprendre	to learn
avoir	to have
commencer	to begin
continuer	to continue
encourager	to encourage
enseigner	to teach
hésiter	to hesitate
inviter	to invite
réussir	to succeed

Note also:

être prêt à	to be ready to
être disposé à	to be willing to
avoir de la difficulté à	to have difficulty in
avoir du mal à	to have difficulty in

Examples:

Je préfère aller me baigner.   I prefer to go for a swim.
Nous espérons aller à la plage cet après-midi.   We hope to go to the beach this afternoon.

Ils ont décidé de louer un pédalo.   They have decided to hire a pedal boat.

Je vous conseille de faire une promenade en bateau.   I advise you to go on a boat trip.

Nous sommes contents de voir le soleil.   We are pleased to see the sun.

Avez-vous réussi à trouver des chaises longues?   Did you succeed in finding some deckchairs?

Nous l'avons aidée à chercher des coquillages (*m.*).   We helped her to look for some shells.

Il est temps de rentrer à l'hôtel.   It's time to return to the hotel.

Vocabulary

l'excursion (*f.*)	excursion
les lunettes (*f.*) **de soleil**	sunglasses
faire du ski nautique	to go water-skiing
faire de la planche à voile	to go wind-surfing

Exercise 55

Complete the following:
1 (I intend to) acheter des lunettes de soleil.
2 (Will it be possible to) faire des excursions?
3 (We prefer to) louer un appartement.
4 (They (*m.*) invited me (*f.*) to) aller à la pêche.
5 (I hesitate to) faire du ski nautique.
6 (Will you have the opportunity to) faire de la planche à voile?

64 Direct object and indirect object pronouns together

Sometimes two object pronouns appear together in the same sentence:

Paul me le donne.   Paul gives it to me.
Nicole nous la vend.   Nicole sells it to us.
Je vous les enverrai.   I'll send them to you.

You will have noticed that **le, la, l', les** follow **me, vous, nous.**

But **le, la, l', les** precede **lui** and **leur:**

Nous le lui avons déjà montré. We have already shown it to him (or to her).
Vous la leur avez donnée? Did you give it to them?
Je ne les lui ai pas vendus. I didn't sell them to him (or to her).

Vocabulary

le dossier	file
le/la collègue	colleague
le télex	telex
la moto	motorbike
la facture	invoice

Exercise 56

Replace all nouns with pronouns (and make any necessary changes):
1 Est-ce que vous m'avez donné le dossier?
2 Notre directeur nous a promis les deux voitures.
3 Mon collègue a l'intention de me vendre ses disques.
4 J'ai envoyé un télex à Paul.
5 Pierre montre sa nouvelle moto à Monique.
6 Nous avons donné les factures aux clients.

65 The pronoun 'en'

En replaces a word or an idea introduced by **de**.
En means:

a) some or any, when not followed by a noun:

Avez-vous des journaux anglais? Do you have any English newspapers?
Oui, nous en avons. Yes, we have some.
Non, nous n'en avons pas. No, we don't have any.

Note that 'some', 'any' must be expressed in French, even if omitted in English:

Avez-vous des enveloppes (*f.*)? Do you have any envelopes?
Oui, j'en ai. Yes, I have.

b) of it, of them:

Avez-vous acheté de l'essence (*f.*)?   Did you buy any petrol?
Oui, j'en ai acheté beaucoup.   Yes, I bought a lot (of it).
Ont-ils des enfants?   Do they have any children?
Oui, ils en ont deux.   Yes, they have two (of them).

c) about it, about them

Avez-vous parlé de la navette spatiale?   Did you talk about (of) the space shuttle?
Oui, tous les astronautes en parlent!   Yes, all the astronauts are talking about it!

d) from there

Est-ce que les ingénieurs vont au centre de contrôle?   Are the engineers going to the control centre?
Non, ils en viennent.   No, they've just come from there. (lit. 'they come from there').

66 The pronoun 'y'

Y replaces a word or an idea introduced by **à**. **Y** means:

a) there:

Est-ce que Paul connaît l'Angleterre?   Does Paul know England?
Oui, il y a passé trois ans.   Yes, he spent three years there.
Est-ce que tu viens de la gare?   Are you (*fam.*) coming from the station?
Non, j'y vais.   No, I'm going there.

Note: when actually pointing, we use **là** or **là-bas**.

b) to it, to them:

Il faut toujours faire la queue à Moscou.   One always has to queue in Moscow.
Oui, mais les Russes y sont habitués.   Yes, but the Russians are used to it.

Note that **y** cannot be omitted:

Est-ce que le directeur est dans son bureau?   Is the director in his office?
Oui, il y est.   Yes, he is.

67 The indefinite pronoun 'on'

In English, when referring to people in general, we use words like
'one', 'they', 'you', 'people' e.g. 'In England people drive on the
left' or 'In China they eat with chopsticks'. In sentences like these the
French use the pronoun **on**, followed by the third person singular of
the verb:

En Angleterre on roule à gauche.   In England they drive on the left.
En Chine on mange avec des baguettes.   In China they eat with
chopsticks.
On dit qu'il parle sept langues.   People say he speaks seven
languages.

On is often used to translate the English passive:

On a invité les diplomates chinois à l'Ambassade de France.   The
Chinese diplomats have been invited to the French Embassy.

Informally in conversation, the French often use **on** in place of **nous**:

Alors, on va partir aujourd'hui ou demain?   Well, are we going to
leave today or tomorrow?

Note: **on** sometimes becomes **l'on** after **et** and **si**; the French find this
sound more pleasant to the ear.

Vocabulary

le banc	bench
l'attitude	attitude
la promotion	promotion
la chance	luck
portatif, portative (*f.*)	portable
sociable	sociable
récemment	recently
encore	again
bien sûr	of course
alors	well
lorsque	when
perfectionner	to perfect
apprécier	to appreciate
s'acheter	to buy for oneself

Irregular verbs:

s'asseoir (to sit down)

Present tense
je m'assieds
tu t'assieds
il/elle s'assied
nous nous asseyons
vous vous asseyez
ils/elles s'asseyent

Perfect tense
je me suis assis, etc

Future tense
je m'assiérai, etc

sortir (to go out)

Present tense
je sors
tu sors
il/elle sort
nous sortons
vous sortez
ils/elles sortent

obtenir (to obtain, to get)

Present tense
j'obtiens
tu obtiens
il/elle obtient
nous obtenons
vous obtenez
ils/elles obtiennent

Perfect tense
j'ai obtenu, etc

Future tense
j'obtiendrai, etc

CONVERSATION

L'anglais en trois mois

David Est-ce que vous vous servez toujours du magnétophone que vous avez acheté récemment?

Isabelle Non, je ne me sers plus de celui-là. Je m'en suis débarrassé et je me suis acheté un magnétophone portatif beaucoup plus perfectionné.

David N'est-il pas difficile d'apprécier la musique avec une si petite machine?

Isabelle Vous vous trompez, ce n'est pas de la musique que j'écoute, ce sont des cassettes d'anglais. Je les ai achetées parce que je dois apprendre l'anglais en trois mois.

David Est-ce que vous avez le temps d'écouter ces cassettes?

Isabelle Oui, bien sûr. Je les écoute le matin lorsque je me lave, lorsque je m'habille, lorsque je me peigne, lorsque je me maquille . . . ce qui prend un certain temps. Mon mari écoute les cassettes aussi quand il se rase, quand il se lave et se brosse les dents. Le dimanche nous aimons sortir et j'écoute encore mes cassettes lorsque nous nous promenons au parc et lorsque nous nous asseyons sur un banc pour nous reposer.

David Ce n'est pas une attitude très sociable.

Isabelle C'est vrai, mais si je réussis à apprendre l'anglais en trois mois, il me sera possible d'obtenir une promotion et de voyager en Angleterre et aux États-Unis.

David Bon, alors, bonne chance ou comme on dit en anglais – 'good luck'!

TRANSLATION

English in three months

David Are you still using the tape recorder you bought recently?

Isabelle No, I'm not using that one any more. I've got rid of it and I've bought myself a much more sophisticated (lit. 'perfected') portable tape recorder.

David Isn't it difficult to appreciate music with such a small machine?

Isabelle You're mistaken, it's not music I listen to, it's English language cassettes (lit. 'cassettes of English'). I bought them because I must learn English in three months.

David   Do you have the time to listen to these cassettes?

Isabelle   Yes, of course. I listen to them in the morning when I'm washing, when I'm getting dressed, when I'm combing my hair, when I'm putting my make-up on . . . which takes a certain amount of time (lit. 'a certain time'). My husband also listens to the cassettes when he's shaving, when he's washing and brushing his teeth.

On Sundays we like to go out and I listen to my cassettes again when we're walking in the park and when we sit down on a bench to rest.

David   That's not a very sociable attitude.

Isabelle   That's true, but if I succeed in learning English in three months, it will be possible for me to get promotion and to travel to England and the United States.

David   Good, well, good luck or as they say in English 'good luck'!

Lesson 11

68 Conjunctions

Study the following:

Reason

parce que	because
car	for, because
puisque	since
comme	as, since
donc	so, therefore

Time

quand	when
lorsque	when
dès que	as soon as
aussitôt que	as soon as
pendant que	while
maintenant que	now that

Contrast

mais	but
tandis que	whereas

Other conjunctions will be discussed in the next lesson.

Examples:

Nous avons acheté une tente, car nous voulons faire du camping.   We have bought a tent, because we want to go camping.
Ma mère n'aime pas les tentes, donc nous avons acheté une caravane.   My mother doesn't like tents, so we've bought a caravan.
Puisque tu es fatigué, nous pourrions camper ici.   Since you're tired, we could camp here.
Pendant que tu vas chercher de l'eau potable, je vais monter la tente.   While you go and get some drinking water, I'll put up the tent.
C'est un bon camping, mais où sont les toilettes?   It's a good campsite, but where are the toilets?

Note that you must use the future tense after **quand, lorsque, dès que** and **aussitôt que** when the future is referred to:

Quand nous ferons du camping l'année prochaine, toute la famille s'amusera bien.   When we go camping next year, the whole family will have a good time.
Aussitôt que tu auras monté la tente, je préparerai à manger.   As soon as you have put up the tent, I'll prepare something to eat.

BUT

Quand je suis en vacances, je dépense toujours beaucoup d'argent.   When (i.e. whenever) I'm on holiday, I always spend a lot of money.

Vocabulary

le lit de camp	camp-bed
le sac de couchage	sleeping bag
le champ	field
la piscine	swimming pool
supplémentaire	extra
tomber en panne	to break down

Exercise 57

Translate:
1 As Paul's friend (*m.*) is coming camping with us, we'll have to buy an extra camp-bed.
2 When you can speak French, we'll go camping in France.
3 Do you take every opportunity to speak French, when you're in Belgium?
4 I don't like this campsite because there's no swimming pool.
5 There are four of us (say 'We are four') but we have only three sleeping bags.
6 The car broke down, so we decided to camp in a field.

69 Numerals over 100

Study the following:

100	**cent**	750	**sept cent cinquante**
101	**cent un**	800	**huit cents**
110	**cent dix**	960	**neuf cent soixante**
150	**cent cinquante**	1000	**mille**
200	**deux cents**	1250	**mille deux cent cinquante**
300	**trois cents**	2000	**deux mille**
400	**quatre cents**	8000	**huit mille**
520	**cinq cent vingt**	9000	**neuf mille**
640	**six cent quarante**	1,000,000	**un million**

Note:

a) **cent** drops the **s** when followed by another number:
   trois cents livres BUT **trois cent quarante livres**

b) When followed by a noun, **un million** takes **de**:
   un million de francs

c) in dates **mille** is sometimes written **mil**:
   en mille (or **mil**) **neuf cent quatre-vingt-six**

Study the following ordinal numbers:

1st	**premier**	8th	**huitième**
2nd	**deuxième**	9th	**neuvième**
3rd	**troisième**	10th	**dixième**
4th	**quatrième**	20th	**vingtième**
5th	**cinquième**	21st	**vingt et unième**
6th	**sixième**	22nd	**vingt-deuxième**
7th	**septième**		

Note:

a) **premier** has a feminine form: **première**

b) **deuxième** has an alternative: **second, seconde** (*f.*)

c) the spelling of **cinquième** and **neuvième**

d) in French we don't say 'Louis the Fourteenth', we say 'Louis fourteen', etc: **Louis quatorze, Henri huit**

Exercise 58

Complete the following, writing the answers in full:

a) 150 + 100 =   d) 450 + 120 =
b) 260 + 40 =   e) 580 + 100 =
c) 320 + 110 =   f) 1000 + 440 =

Vocabulary

le casino	casino
le concert	concert
le ballet	ballet
l'opéra (*m.*)	opera
la discothèque	disco
la boîte de nuit	night club
la patinoire	skating rink

Exercise 59

Translate:
 1 the first disco
 2 the second casino
 3 the third night club
 4 the fourth theatre
 5 the fifth concert
 6 the sixth opera
 7 the seventh cinema
 8 the eighth skating rink
 9 the ninth ballet
10 the tenth restaurant

70 The passive voice

The passive is formed, as in English, with the verb **être** and the past participle which agrees with the subject; 'by' is translated **par**:

Un tunnel sera construit sous la Manche.   A tunnel will be built under the Channel.
Le traité a été signé par les deux gouvernements.   The treaty has been signed by both governments.

'By' is sometimes translated **de**, especially after verbs of feeling:

La Reine est respectée de tout le monde. The Queen is respected by everyone.

The French have a tendency to avoid the passive and do so in one of the following ways:

a) by using the pronoun **on** (see Lesson 10):

> **On a déjà oublié le tunnel que les Britanniques ont annulé en 1975.** The tunnel which the British cancelled in 1975 has already been forgotten.

Be careful with those verbs which take an indirect object like **donner à** (to give to), **dire à** (to tell, to say to), **répondre à** (to reply to, to answer), **demander à** (to ask), because although we can say in English 'I've been given', 'he's been told', 'the letter has been answered', 'she's been asked' etc. this construction is impossible in French and you must use **on**:

> **On m'a dit qu'il y aura un train toutes les trois minutes.** I've been told that there will be a train every three minutes.
> **On lui a demandé ce qu'il pensait du projet.** He was asked what he thought of the project.
> **On a déjà répondu à la lettre.** The letter has already been answered.

b) by changing the roles of subject and agent and using the active voice:

> **La construction d'un lien fixe trans-Manche créera beaucoup d'emplois.** Many jobs will be created by the building of a cross-Channel fixed link.

c) by occasionally using a reflexive verb:

> **Cela ne se vend pas en France.**
> That's not sold in France.

Vocabulary

le continent	continent
la traversée	crossing
la république	republic
la décision	decision
l'importance (*f.*)	importance
ferroviaire	rail
routier, routière (*f.*)	road
historique	historic
étranger, étrangère (*f.*)	foreign
relier	to link
annoncer	to announce
souligner	to emphasize

Irregular verb:

construire (to build)

Present tense
je construis
tu construis
il/elle construit
nous construisons
vous construisez
ils/elles construisent

Perfect tense
j'ai construit, etc

Exercise 60

Change the following into the passive:
1 Le président de la République française a souligné l'importance de la décision.
2 Un tunnel ferroviaire reliera la Grande-Bretagne au continent en 1993.
3 On construira plus tard un lien routier.
4 On a annoncé cette décision historique à Lille.
5 La traversée de la Manche a souvent découragé les touristes étrangers.

71 The present participle

The present participle in English ends in -ing, and it is often preceded by 'while', 'on', 'by', 'in'; in French it ends in **-ant** and is often preceded by **en**:

Il s'est cassé la jambe, en jouant au football.   He broke his leg while playing football.

En étudiant un peu tous les jours, vous apprendrez le français en trois mois.   By studying a little every day, you will learn French in three months.

The present participle can be used, as in English, without a preceding preposition:

Voyant que le patron était de bonne humeur, il a demandé une augmentation de salaire.   Seeing that the boss was in a good mood, he asked for an increase in salary.

The present participle is formed by removing the **-ons** from the first person plural of the present tense and adding **-ant**:

chantant	singing
finissant	finishing
vendant	selling
écrivant	writing

There are three exceptions; **avoir, être** and **savoir**:

ayant	having
étant	being
sachant	knowing

Remember that **en** is the only preposition that is followed by the present participle in French; all others are followed by the infinitive (see Lesson 10).

Remember also that sentences such as 'I am going', 'I am watching', 'I am listening' are translated by the present tense (see Lesson 2):

je vais
je regarde
j'écoute

Vocabulary

le bras	arm
le cours	course, class
le diplôme	diploma
l'agent de police	policeman
la fois	time, occasion
la réponse	reply
blessé	injured
par	per
faire du ski	to ski
tomber	to fall (conjugated with **être**)
patiner	to skate
appeler	to call (see lesson 12)

Irregular verb:

voir (to see)

Present tense
je vois
tu vois
il/elle voit
nous voyons
vous voyez
ils/elles voient

Perfect tense
j'ai vu, etc

Exercise 61

Combine the following using a present participle:
1 Elle s'est cassé le bras. Elle faisait du ski.
2 Je suis tombé. Je patinais.
3 Il allait aux cours du soir trois fois par semaine. Il a obtenu son diplôme.
4 L'agent de police a vu que l'automobiliste était blessé. Il a appelé une ambulance.
5 Vous téléphonez. Vous aurez la réponse tout de suite.

72 More about the imperative

The imperative of **avoir** and **être** is:

aie	have (*fam.*)	**sois**	be (*fam.*)
ayez	have	**soyez**	be
ayons	let's have	**soyons**	let's be

Examples:

Ayez un peu de patience.   Have a little patience.
Ne soyez pas en retard.   Don't be late.
Soyons raisonnables.   Let's be reasonable.

73 The imperative with pronouns

Study the following:

Invitez votre secrétaire au restaurant.   Invite your secretary to the restaurant.
Invitez-la.   Invite her.
Ne l'invitez pas.   Don't invite her.

Donnez le numéro de téléphone aux clients.   Give the telephone number to the clients.
Donnez-leur le numéro.   Give them the number.
Ne leur donnez pas le numéro.   Don't give them the number.

Asseyez-vous dans ce fauteuil.   Sit down in this armchair.
Ne vous asseyez pas dans ce fauteuil.   Don't sit down in this armchair.

You will have noticed that:

a) pronouns follow the verb in the affirmative imperative.
b) pronouns precede the verb in the negative imperative.

Study the following:

Donnez-moi votre adresse.
Donnez-la-moi.
Ne me donnez pas votre adresse.
Ne me la donnez pas.
Couche-toi.
Ne te couche pas.

You will have noticed that:

a) **me** and **te** become **moi** and **toi** in the affirmative imperative.
b) in the affirmative imperative we say **donnez-le-moi,**
   envoyez-la-moi, montrez-les-moi.

Remember, of course, that an imperative can be made more polite by putting one of the following expressions in front of the infinitive:

Voulez-vous . . .?   Will you . . .?
Voulez-vous bien . . .? Would you kindly . . .?
Pourriez-vous . . .?   Could you . . .?

Examples:

Voulez-vous signer ici, s'il vous plaît?   Will you sign here please?
Voulez-vous bien passer à la caisse, s'il vous plaît?   Would you kindly go to the cashdesk please?
Pourriez-vous nous apporter encore du café?   Could you bring us some more coffee?

Vocabulary

le catalogue	catalogue
l'échantillon (*m.*)	sample
la brochure	brochure
faire des heures (*f.*) **supplémentaires**	to work overtime

Exercise 62

Imagine you're asking your secretary to carry out a number of tasks. The trouble is you keep changing your mind!

Translate:
1 Telephone him – no, don't telephone him.
2 Send them this brochure – no, don't send it to them.
3 Copy this document – no, don't copy it.
4 Give me the catalogue – no, don't give it to me.
5 Send her the samples – no, don't send them to her.
6 Type this letter – no, don't type it.
7 Be here at 9 o'clock – no, at 8 o'clock.
8 Would you be so kind as to work overtime?

74 The pluperfect

'I had telephoned', 'I had spoken' etc. is expressed by using the imperfect of **avoir** or **être** with the past participle:

J'avais déjà téléphoné à l'hôpital.   I had already telephoned the hospital.
Elle était déjà partie, quand son mari est arrivé.   She had already left, when her husband arrived.

75 'Depuis' (since)

The French sometimes use the present tense where we use the past tense in English. This happens when an action, which began in the past, is still continuing in the present:

Depuis quand êtes-vous en France?   How long have you been in France? (lit. 'Since when are you in France?')
Depuis combien de temps apprenez-vous le français?   How long have you been learning French?
Je suis en France depuis une semaine, mais j'apprends le français depuis trois mois.   I've been in France for a week, but I've been learning French for three months.

76 'Venir de' (to have just . . .)

This idiomatic expression, used only in the present and imperfect tenses, expresses the idea of 'having just done something'.

Je viens d'acheter une maison.   I have just bought a house.
Elle venait de vendre son appartement.   She had just sold her flat.

Vocabulary

le docteur	doctor
le pompier	fireman
l'ambulancier	ambulance driver
le permis de conduire	driving licence
jouer du piano	to play the piano
prévenir	to inform (conjugated like **venir**)
transporter	to transport

Exercise 63

Translate:

1 I've been married for five years.
2 I've lived in this house for four years.
3 I've worked for this bank for three years.
4 I've had this car for two years.
5 I've been learning to play the piano for one year.

Exercise 64

Answer the questions as follows:

Allez-vous téléphoner à la police?   Are you going to telephone the
police?
Mais je viens de téléphoner à la police.   But I've just telephoned the
police.

1 Allez-vous appeler un docteur?
2 Allez-vous prévenir les pompiers?
3 Pouvez-vous me montrer votre permis de conduire?
4 Est-ce que les ambulanciers vont transporter les blessés à l'hôpital?
5 Est-ce que vous allez me donner votre adresse?

Vocabulary

le volant	steering wheel
le rêve	dream
le moment	moment
le projet	project
l'isolement (*m.*)	isolation
la nouvelle	news
la liaison	link
la fin	end
l'île (*f.*)	island
la façon	way
l'entente (*f.*)	understanding
nécessaire	necessary
contre	against
cordial	cordial
jurer	to swear
réaliser	to realise
vive	long live

> Irregular verb:
>
> **vivre** (to live)
>
> *Present tense*
> **je vis**
> **tu vis**
> **il/elle vit**
> **nous vivons**
> **vous vivez**
> **ils/elles vivent**
>
> *Perfect tense*
> **j'ai vécu,** etc

CONVERSATION

Le tunnel sous la Manche

Une conversation entre un Anglais et une Française

Anglais   On vient d'annoncer une grande nouvelle. La décision a été prise de construire un tunnel ferroviaire sous la Manche!

Française   Vraiment? Depuis le temps qu'on en parle! Un tunnel ferroviaire, vous dites? Mais le premier ministre britannique avait juré qu'elle serait la première à traverser la Manche au volant de sa voiture.

Anglais   Oui, c'est vrai, mais aussitôt que la liaison routière sera construite, elle pourra réaliser son rêve.

Française   À ce moment-là elle ne sera peut-être plus premier ministre! Qu'est-ce que vous pensez vous-même du projet?

Anglais   Eh bien, en prenant cette décision, on met fin à l'isolement de la Grande-Bretagne, ce qui est nécessaire si on veut vivre au vingtième siècle, et en même temps on créera de nouveaux emplois.

Française   Y a-t-il des gens qui sont contre le projet?

Anglais   Oui, il y a des gens qui pensent que la Grande-Bretagne devrait rester une île. Ils ont peut-être raison.

Française   Oui, peut-être, mais de toutes façons, avec un tunnel ou sans tunnel – vive l'Entente cordiale!

TRANSLATION

The Tunnel under the Channel

A conversation between an Englishman and a Frenchwoman

Englishman	An important piece of news (lit. 'a big news') has just been announced. The decision has been taken to build a rail tunnel under the Channel!
Frenchwoman	Really? They've been talking about it for a long time! (lit. 'Since the time one is talking about it!'). A rail tunnel, you say? But the British Prime Minister swore (lit. 'had sworn') that she would be the first to cross the Channel at the wheel of her car.
Englishman	Yes, it's true, but as soon as the road link is built (lit. 'will be built'), she'll be able to realise her dream.
Frenchwoman	Then she may no longer be Prime Minister! What do you yourself think about the project?
Englishman	Well, by taking this decision, they are putting an end to Britain's isolation, which is necessary if we want to live in the twentieth century, and at the same time they are creating new jobs.
Frenchwoman	Are there people who are against the project?
Englishman	Yes, there are some people who think that Britain should remain an island. Perhaps they're right.
Frenchwoman	Yes, perhaps, but in any case (lit. 'of all ways'), with a tunnel or without a tunnel – long live the Entente Cordiale!

Lesson 12

77 The verb faire

Faire is the most overworked verb in the French language. It is conjugated as follows:

Present tense

je fais	**nous faisons**
tu fais	**vous faites**
il/elle fait	**ils/elles font**

Perfect tense
j'ai fait

Imperfect tense
je faisais

Future tense
je ferai

Faire can have a variety of meanings, as shown in the following examples.

a) to do:
Qu'est-ce que vous faites dans la vie?   What do you do for a living?

b) to make:
Ma mère va faire un gâteau.   My mother is going to make a cake.

c) to give:
Je vais faire une conférence sur la graphologie.   I'm going to give a lecture on graphology.

d) to take:
Elle aime faire une promenade au parc.   She likes to take a walk in the park.

e) to have:
Mon mari fait de la tension.   My husband has high blood pressure.

f) to act:
Ne fais pas l'idiot.   Don't act the fool.

g) to force:
Je l'ai fait travailler.   I forced him to work (or I made him work).

h) to have something done:
Ils font construire une maison.   They're having a house built.

i) it is used to talk about the weather (see Lessson 6):
Il fait beau.   The weather is fine.

j) it is used in many idiomatic expressions:
Tu me fais marcher.   You're pulling my leg.

Vocabulary

la profession	profession
la tarte	tart
la pomme	apple
la psychologie	psychology
la fièvre	fever
bête	silly

Exercise 65

Rewrite the following using the verb faire:
1 Quelle est votre profession?
2 Ma soeur prépare une tarte aux pommes.
3 Je vais parler de la psychologie devant 200 personnes.
4 Elle s'est promenée au parc hier.
5 Il a de la fièvre.
6 Ne sois pas bête.
7 J'ai forcé mon fils à travailler.
8 On me construit une maison à Avignon.

78 The past historic

There is a past tense that you will meet when reading books, magazines and newspapers, but almost never in conversation, which is called the past historic or past definite. It is a literary tense and you yourself will never need to use it, but you must be able to recognise it.

The past historic describes a completed action in the past and, in the case of regular verbs, is formed by removing the **-er**, **-ir**, **-re** from the infinitive and adding the following endings:

-er verbs		**-ir/-re** verbs	
je	-ai	je	-is
tu	-as	tu	-is
il/elle	-a	il/elle	-it
nous	-âmes	nous	-îmes
vous	-âtes	vous	-îtes
ils/elles	-èrent	ils/elles	-irent

Examples:

Le lendemain Paul arriva tôt.   The following day Paul arrived early.
Les touristes visitèrent cinq pays en cinq jours.   The tourists visited five countries in five days.
Victor Hugo finit d'écrire Les Misérables en 1862.   Victor Hugo finished writing Les Misérables in 1862.

79 The past historic of irregular verbs

You will sometimes be able to recognise the past historic of irregular verbs by the similarity to the past participle:

Infinitive	Perfect tense	Past historic	Meaning
dire	**j'ai dit**	**je dis**	I said
mettre	**j'ai mis**	**je mis**	I put
prendre	**j'ai pris**	**je pris**	I took
sortir	**je suis sorti**	**je sortis**	I went out
avoir	**j'ai eu**	**j'eus**	I had
lire	**j'ai lu**	**je lus**	I read
vivre	**j'ai vécu**	**je vécus**	I lived

Other irregular forms just have to be learned:

écrire	**j'ai écrit**	**j'écrivis**	I wrote
être	**j'ai été**	**je fus**	I was
faire	**j'ai fait**	**je fis**	I did
venir	**je suis venu**	**je vins**	I came
voir	**j'ai vu**	**je vis**	I saw

Exercise 66

Translate into English:
1 Il donna.
2 Je vendis.
3 Nous finîmes.
4 Elle eut.
5 Je fus.
6 Vous eûtes.
7 Il prit.
8 Elle sortit.
9 Ils lurent.
10 Elles mirent.

80 Verbs requiring a preposition in English, but not in French, and vice versa

Although a preposition is necessary in English to complete the meaning of the following English verbs, none is required in French:

to approve of	**approuver**
to listen to	**écouter**
to look at	**regarder**
to look for	**chercher**
to ask for	**demander**
to pay for	**payer**
to wait for	**attendre**

Conversely, a preposition is sometimes needed in French but not in English:

demander à	to ask
dire à	to tell
défendre à	to forbid
obéir à	to obey
permettre à	to allow
ressembler à	to resemble
toucher à	to touch
jouer à	to play (game)
jouer de	to play (instrument)

Examples:

J'ai écouté les explications du guide avec attention.   I listened carefully to the guide's explanations.
Regardez la cathédrale à droite.   Look at the cathedral on the right.
Attendez les autres membres du groupe.   Wait for the other members of the group.
Nous cherchons les toilettes.   We are looking for the toilets.
Je vais demander deux billets d'entrée.   I'm going to ask for two admission tickets.
Il aime jouer au tennis.   He likes to play tennis.
Elle aime jouer du piano.   She likes to play the piano.

81 Spelling changes

In French, a verb can only be regarded as regular if its basic sound remains the same throughout the conjugation. In order to retain this basic sound, we sometimes have to make changes in the spelling. Let's take an example:

We have learned that we form the present tense by removing the **-er** from the infinitive and adding certain endings, and in the case of **nous** we add **-ons.** But if we do this with the verb **manger** (to eat), pronounced 'mah*ng*-zhay', we will have 'mangons', pronounced 'mah*ng*-go*ng*' i.e. a change in the basic sound. So, in order to keep the soft sound 'zh' we must add an e and we write **nous mangeons.** This spelling change takes place whenever the **g** is followed by **o** or **a:**

nous mangeons	we eat	(present tense)
je mangeais	I was eating	(imperfect)
il mangea	he ate	(past historic)
en mangeant	while eating	(present participle)

Here are some important verbs that behave like **manger:**

arranger	to arrange
corriger	to correct
décourager	to discourage
encourager	to encourage
déranger	to disturb
nager	to swim
voyager	to travel

Everything that has been said about keeping the **g** soft also applies to the soft **c** in a verb like **annoncer** (to announce). In order to keep the **c** soft in the nous-form, we have to add a cedilla (ی) to the **c** and we write **nous annonçons**. If we don't do this, the pronunciation will be 'ah-no*ng*-ko*ng*'. So, we write **ç** before **o** and **a**:

nous annonçons	we announce
j'annonçais	I was announcing
il annonça	he announced
en annonçant	while announcing

Important verbs like **annoncer**:

commencer	to begin
divorcer	to divorce
prononcer	to pronounce
remplacer	to replace

Some verbs whose infinitive ends in **-eler** and **-eter** double the **l** and **t** before a silent **e**:

appeler (to call)

Present tense

j'appelle	**nous appelons**
tu appelles	**vous appelez**
il/elle appelle	**ils/elles appellent**

Future tense
j'appellerai

Conditional tense
j'appellerais

Important verbs like **appeler**:

rappeler	to call back, to remind
renouveler	to renew
jeter	to throw

Some verbs change **e** to **è** before a silent **e**:

acheter (to buy)

Present tense

j'achète	**nous achetons**
tu achètes	**vous achetez**
il/elle achète	**ils/elles achètent**

Future tense
j'achèterai

Conditional tense
j'achèterais

Important verbs like **acheter:**

lever	to raise
se lever	to get up
mener	to lead
amener	to bring

Some verbs change **é** to **è** before a silent **e** (present tense and present subjunctive only):

espérer (to hope)

Present tense

j'espère	**nous espérons**
tu espères	**vous espérez**
il/elle espère	**ils/elles espèrent**

Important verbs like **espérer:**

considérer	to consider
régler	to settle
répéter	to repeat
s'inquiéter	to worry
préférer	to prefer

Verbs whose infinitive ends in **-yer** change **y** to **i** before a silent **e**:

nettoyer (to clean)

Present tense

je nettoie	**nous nettoyons**
tu nettoies	**vous nettoyez**
il/elle nettoie	**ils/elles nettoient**

Future tense
je nettoierai

Conditional tense
je nettoierais

Important verbs like **nettoyer:**

employer	to use
s'ennuyer	to be bored
envoyer	to send
(*Future:* **j'enverrai**)	
payer	to pay (optional spelling change)
essayer	to try (optional spelling change)

82 The subjunctive

We have a subjunctive mood in English, although it is used much less often than in French. In English, when we make a suggestion or express a wish, we use the subjunctive. For example, when we say 'I suggest that a vote be taken' or 'I wish today were Saturday', 'be' and 'were' are subjunctives.

In French, we use the subjunctive after verbs and expressions which denote:

a)	a wish	**vouloir, désirer**	to want, to wish
b)	a preference	**préférer**	to prefer
c)	a suggestion	**suggérer, proposer**	to suggest
d)	a necessity	**falloir**	to be necessary
e)	a demand	**exiger**	to demand
f)	surprise	**être surpris**	to be surprised
g)	regret	**regretter**	to regret
h)	anger	**être furieux**	to be furious
i)	fear	**avoir peur**	to be afraid
j)	doubt	**douter**	to doubt
k)	possibility	**être possible**	to be possible
l)	pleasure	**être content**	to be pleased
m)	sorrow	**être désolé**	to be sorry

The subjunctive is always preceded by the conjunction **que** (that).

The subjunctive is formed by removing the **-ent** ending from the third person plural form of the present tense and adding:

je	-e	**nous**	-ions
tu	-es	**vous**	-iez
il/elle	-e	**ils/elles**	-ent

Examples:

. . .que je parle   . . .que nous vendions
. . .que tu donnes   . . .que vous répondiez
. . .qu'il finisse   . . .qu'ils mettent
. . .qu'elle maigrisse   . . .qu'elles permettent

Examples of the use of the subjunctive:

Je voudrais que vous me fixiez un rendez-vous chez le coiffeur.
I would like you to fix an appointment for me at the hairdresser's.
Je voudrais que vous me coupiez les cheveux. I would like you to
cut my hair.
Je préfère qu'il ne me coupe pas les cheveux trop court. I prefer
him not to cut my hair too short.
Je veux qu'il me rase. I want him to shave me.
Il faut que vous me mettiez un peu de laque (*f.*) **sur les cheveux à
cause du vent.** You must put a little hair spray on my hair because
of the wind.
Je suis surpris(e) que le coiffeur ne vende pas de peignes (*m.*).
I am surprised that the hairdresser doesn't sell combs.
Je suis content(e) que vous me parliez en français. I am pleased
that you are talking to me in French.

It is important to note that when the subject of the dependent verb is
the same as that of the main verb, the construction with an infinitive is
used. Compare:

Je voudrais partir. I'd like to leave.
Nous voudrions partir. We'd like to leave.

BUT

Nous voudrions que vous partiez. We'd like you to leave.

There are some irregular subjunctives and the most important are:

être (to be)	**que je sois, il soit, nous soyons, ils soient**
avoir (to have)	**que j'aie, il ait, nous ayons, ils aient**
aller (to go)	**que j'aille, il aille, nous allions, ils aillent**
faire (to do, make)	**que je fasse, il fasse, nous fassions, ils fassent**
pouvoir (to be able)	**que je puisse, il puisse, nous puissions, ils puissent**
prendre (to take)	**que je prenne, il prenne, nous prenions, ils prennent**

savoir (to know)	**que je sache, il sache, nous sachions, ils sachent**
venir (to come)	**que je vienne, il vienne, nous venions, ils viennent**

The subjunctive is also used after the following conjunctions:

quoique	although	**à condition que**	on condition that
bien que	although	**pourvu que**	provided that
pour que	in order that	**jusqu'à ce que**	until
afin que	in order that	**à moins que★**	unless
de peur que★	for fear that	**avant que★**	before

★In addition to taking the subjunctive, these conjunctions require **ne** before the verb.

Examples:

Bien qu'il sache parler français, il refuse de téléphoner à Paris.   Although he can speak French, he refuses to telephone Paris.
J'ai acheté ce poste de radio pour que vous puissiez écouter les émissions françaises.   I've bought this radio set so that you can listen to French broadcasts.
Je veux bien vous donner les cassettes, à condition que vous étudiiez chaque soir.   I'm quite willing to give you the cassettes, on condition that you study every evening.
À moins que vous ne m'aidiez, je ne pourrai pas finir cet exercice.   Unless you help me, I won't be able to finish this exercise.
Je dois rester ici jusqu'à ce que ma femme arrive.   I must stay here until my wife arrives.

The subjunctive is also used after:

a) a superlative:

C'est la plus grande librairie que nous ayons jamais vue.   This is the biggest bookshop we have ever seen.

b) **seul** (only), **premier** (first), **dernier** (last):

Paul est le seul qui puisse aller à la réunion.   Paul is the only one who can go to the meeting.

c) an indefinite antecedent:

Je cherche un médecin qui sache parler anglais.   I'm looking for a doctor who can speak English. (I'm not sure that one exists)

BUT

Je cherche le médecin qui sait parler anglais.   I'm looking for the doctor who can speak English. (I know he exists)

d) impersonal verbs such as:

Il faut que . . .	It is necessary that . . .
Il vaut mieux que . . .	It is better that . . .
Il est important que . . .	It is important that . . .
Il est possible que . . .	It is possible that . . .
Il est inévitable que . . .	It is inevitable that . . .
Il est dommage que . . .	It is a pity that . . .

Examples:

Il est important que nous réservions les chambres à l'avance.   It is important that we reserve the rooms in advance.
Il est dommage qu'il ne vienne pas aujourd'hui.   It is a pity that he's not coming today.

e) the negative of **penser** (to think) and **croire** (to believe). Compare:

Je pense que Caroline va à la réception.   I think that Caroline is going to the reception.
Je ne pense pas que Caroline aille à la réception.   I don't think Caroline is going to the reception.

f) **quoi que** (whatever):

. . .**quoi que vous fassiez . . .**   . . . whatever you do . . .

g) **quel que, quelle que, quels que, quelles que** (whatever):

. . .**quelle que soit la raison . . .**   . . . whatever the reason may be . . .

The subjunctive is also used for the third person imperative:

Qu'il prenne le parapluie.   Let him take the umbrella.
Qu'elle parte.   Let her leave.
Qu'ils fassent la vaisselle.   Let them do the washing-up.

Note that there is also a perfect subjunctive which is used for action in the past. The perfect subjunctive is formed with **avoir** or **être**:

Je suis content que vous ayez retrouvé votre portefeuille (*m.*)   I am pleased that you have found your wallet.
Je suis désolé qu'elle soit tombée malade.   I am sorry that she has fallen ill.

Vocabulary

le lancement	launching
le vaisseau spatial	spacecraft
le discours	speech
l'espace (*m.*)	space
la déclaration	statement
la conquête	conquest
la mission	mission
l'apesanteur (*f.*)	weightlessness
l'expérience (*f.*)	experiment, experience
les données (*f.*)	data
continuer	to continue
participer	to take part
filmer	to film
enregistrer	to record
reporter	to postpone
mener	to conduct
avoir lieu	to take place
en direct	live
quand même	still, nevertheless

Exercise 67

Translate:
1 I suggest that the President make a statement on television.
2 We must continue our conquest of space.
3 He would like the launching of the spacecraft to take place next week.
4 I am pleased that you are taking part in this space mission.
5 It is important that the launching should be filmed live.
6 Unless you can give me all the data recorded by the computers, I cannot take a decision.

7 We are pleased that the President has decided to postpone his speech.
8 Although the astronauts are used to weightlessness, they still have a little difficulty carrying out their experiments on board the spacecraft.

Vocabulary

le/la graphologue	graphologist
le mariage	wedding, marriage
le(s) renseignement(s) (*m.*)	information
l'échantillon (*m.*)	sample
la conversation téléphonique	telephone conversation
la personnalité	personality
la conclusion	conclusion
l'écriture (*f.*)	handwriting
l'analyse (*f.*)	analysis
les félicitations (*f.*)	congratulations
analyser	analyse
rédiger	to write, compose
retarder	to delay
tout à fait	quite, completely
compatible	compatible
ordinaire	ordinary
favorable	favourable
alors	so
allô	hallo (on the telephone)

CONVERSATION

Une conversation téléphonique entre un graphologue et une jeune cliente

Cliente Allô. Bonjour, Monsieur. C'est vous le graphologue?
Graphologue Oui, c'est moi.
Cliente Eh bien, mon fiancé vient de fixer la date de notre mariage et . . .
Graphologue Félicitations, Mademoiselle!
Cliente Merci. Je ne crois pas que je sois tout à fait prête pour le

mariage, alors je voudrais que vous analysiez mon écriture et aussi celle de mon fiancé pour voir si nos personnalités sont compatibles.

Graphologue Oui, c'est très facile. Il faut que vous m'envoyiez un échantillon de votre écriture et de celle de votre fiancé.

Cliente Quelle sorte d'échantillon faut-il que je vous envoie?

Graphologue Je préfère que vous écriviez une lettre tout à fait ordinaire, mais il faut qu'elle soit signée.

Cliente Je doute que mon fiancé soit prêt à rédiger une lettre et à la signer sans savoir pourquoi.

Graphologue Mais il est très important qu'il n'en connaisse pas la raison.

Cliente Bon, très bien. Pour que vous puissiez arriver à une conclusion plus rapidement, est-ce qu'il faut que nous vous donnions des renseignements supplémentaires?

Graphologue Non, pas du tout.

Cliente Vous savez, cette analyse est très importante pour moi. À moins que votre rapport ne soit favorable, il est possible que je retarde le mariage.

TRANSLATION

A telephone conversation between a graphologist and a young client

Client Hallo. Good morning. Are you the graphologist?

Graphologist Yes, I am.

Client Well, my fiancé has just fixed the date of our wedding and . . .

Graphologist Congratulations!

Client Thank you. I don't think I'm quite ready for marriage, so I would like you to analyse my handwriting and also my fiancé's in order to see if our personalities are compatible.

Graphologist Yes, that's very easy. You must send me a sample of your handwriting and your fiancé's.

Client What sort of sample must I send you?

Graphologist I prefer you to write a perfectly ordinary letter, but it must be signed.

Client I doubt whether my fiancé will be willing to write a letter and to sign it without knowing why.

Graphologist	But it's very important that he doesn't know the reason for it.
Client	OK, fine. So that you can come to a conclusion more rapidly, must we give you any additional information?
Graphologist	No, not at all.
Client	You know, this analysis is very important for me. Unless your report is favourable, it's possible I may delay the wedding.

Exercise 68

Translate back into French all the English translations of the CONVERSATIONS which have appeared in this book.

Exercise 69

Translate back into French all the English translations of the EXAMPLES which have appeared in this book.

Exercise 70

Translate back into French all the English translations of the VOCABULARY LISTS which have appeared in this book.

Exercise 71

Translate back into English all the sentences in the KEY TO EXERCISES.

Reading Practice

These extracts from French literature and modern journals each have an English translation on the facing page. Refer to this as little as possible during your first reading of the French, then go through the piece again, noting constructions and vocabulary.

Les Misérables

L'hôpital était une maison étroite et basse à un seul étage avec un petit jardin.

Trois jours après son arrivée, l'évêque visita l'hôpital. La visite terminée, il fit prier le directeur de vouloir bien venir jusque chez lui.

—Monsieur le directeur de l'hôpital, lui dit-il, combien en ce moment avez-vous de malades?

—Vingt-six, monseigneur.

—C'est ce que j'avais compté, dit l'évêque.

—Les lits, reprit le directeur, sont bien serrés les uns contre les autres.

—C'est ce que j'avais remarqué.

—Les salles ne sont que des chambres et l'air s'y renouvelle difficilement.

—C'est ce qui me semble.

—Et puis, quand il y a un rayon de soleil, le jardin est bien petit pour les convalescents.

—C'est bien ce que je me disais.

—Dans les épidémies, nous avons eu cette année le typhus, nous avons eu la suette militaire il y a deux ans; cent malades quelquefois, nous ne savons que faire.

—C'est la pensée qui m'était venue.

—Que voulez-vous, monseigneur? dit le directeur, il faut se résigner.

Les Misérables

The hospital was a narrow and low two-storeyed house with a small garden.

Three days after his arrival, the bishop visited the hospital. When the visit was over, he asked the director to be good enough to come home with him.

'Director,' he said to him, 'how many patients do you have at this moment?'

'Twenty six, Monseigneur.'

'That's how many I counted,' said the bishop.

'The beds,' continued the director, 'are very close to each other.'

'I noticed.'

'The wards are only bedrooms and the air is not very fresh.'

'I can imagine.'

'And when we do get some sunshine, the garden is very small for the convalescents.'

'That's what I was thinking.'

'When we have an epidemic, this year we've had typhus and two years ago we had military fever, with up to a hundred patients sometimes, we don't know what to do.'

'That thought had occurred to me.'

'What can one do, Monseigneur?' said the director. 'We must resign ourselves to it.'

Cette conversation avait lieu dans la salle à manger-galerie du rez-de-chaussée.

L'évêque garda un moment de silence, puis il se tourna brusquement vers le directeur de l'hôpital.

–Monsieur, dit-il, combien pensez-vous qu'il tiendrait de lits rien que dans cette salle?

–Dans la salle à manger de monseigneur? s'écria le directeur stupéfait.

L'évêque parcourait la salle du regard et semblait y faire avec les yeux des mesures et des calculs.

–Il y tiendrait bien vingt lits! dit-il, comme se parlant à lui-même, puis élevant la voix:

–Tenez, monsieur le directeur de l'hôpital, je vais vous dire. Il y a évidemment une erreur. Vous êtes vingt-six personnes dans cinq ou six petites chambres. Nous sommes trois ici et nous avons place pour soixante, il y a erreur, je vous dis, vous avez mon logis et j'ai le vôtre. Rendez-moi ma maison; c'est ici chez vous.

Le lendemain les vingt-six pauvres malades étaient installés dans le palais de l'évêque et l'évêque était à l'hôpital.

Taken from Book 1, Chapter 2   Victor Hugo (1802–1885)

This conversation took place in the ground floor banquet-hall.

The bishop remained silent for a moment, then he suddenly turned towards the director of the hospital.

'Tell me,' he said, 'how many beds do you think this room would hold?'

'The Monseigneur's dining room?' the director cried out, astonished.

The bishop looked around the room and seemed to be taking measurements and making calculations with his eyes.

'It would certainly hold twenty beds,' he said, as if talking to himself. Then he raised his voice:

'Listen, Director, I'm going to tell you something. There's obviously an error. You have twenty six people in five or six small bedrooms. There are three of us here and we have room for sixty. There's an error, I tell you. You have my house and I have yours. Give me back my house. You should be here.'

The following day the twenty six poor patients were installed in the bishop's palace and the bishop was installed in the hospital.

Tunnel sous la Manche en 1993

France–Angleterre
en une demi-heure

Paris à trois heures de Londres par le T.G.V.

Le premier ministre britannique et le président de la République française ont choisi: la France et l'Angleterre seront reliées, en 1993, par un tunnel ferroviaire à deux tubes, assorti d'une galerie de service. Les véhicules, pour traverser la Manche, devront donc prendre place sur des navettes. Mme Thatcher, semble-t-il, aurait préféré, à côté d'un tunnel pour les trains, un lien routier autonome.

C'est donc le projet du consortium franco-britannique France-Manche/Channel Tunnel Group qui a été retenu. Cependant, les deux gouvernements ont demandé à ses responsables de déposer un projet de liaison routière destiné à compléter l'ensemble ferroviaire d'ici à quinze ans. Faute de présenter un tel projet, l'exclusivité de la concession accordée sera perdue, a dit François Mitterrand.

Le 12 février, à Londres, sera signée la convention entre les deux États. Après ratification par les Parlements d'ici à un an, les travaux pourraient commencer à la mi-1987 pour une mise en service en 1993. Coût total de l'ouvrage: 53 milliards de francs.

Les navettes partiront toutes les trois minutes en période de pointe. Trafic possible: quatre mille voitures par heure dans chaque sens. La durée du parcours, long de quelque 50 kilomètres, sera de vingt-six minutes à une vitesse maximale de 160 km/h. Il ne s'agit là bien sûr que de la traversée du tunnel lui-même. La durée totale du trajet ferroviaire Paris-Londres sera de quatre heures trente minutes en 1993; de trois heures quand le T.G.V. sera en service.

Trafic voyageurs prévu en l'an 2000 entre les deux pays: quarante-cinq millions de passagers répartis entre tous les moyens de transport.

From Le Figaro 21.1.1986

Tunnel under the Channel in 1993

France-England
in half an hour

Paris – three hours from London by high-speed train.

The British Prime Minister and the President of the French Republic have made their choice: France and England will be linked, in 1993, by a twin-rail tunnel, equipped with a service tunnel. Vehicles will therefore have to be placed on shuttle trains for the Channel crossing. Mrs Thatcher, apparently, would have preferred an independent road link alongside the rail tunnel.

So, it is the project submitted by the Franco-British consortium France-Manche/Channel Tunnel Group which has been accepted. However, both governments have asked the consortium's management to submit a proposal for a road link to complete the rail complex within fifteen years. If it fails to submit such a proposal, the exclusive rights granted will be lost, said François Mitterrand.

This agreement between the two countries will be signed on the 12th February in London. After ratification by the Parliaments within a year, work could begin mid-1987 and the scheme could be in operation in 1993. Total cost of the work will be 53 thousand million francs.

The shuttles will leave every three minutes at peak periods. Potential traffic is four thousand cars per hour in each direction. The duration of the journey, some 50 kilometres, will be 26 minutes at a maximum speed of 160 km per hour. Of course, this refers only to the passage through the tunnel itself. The total duration of the rail journey Paris-London will be four hours thirty minutes in 1993, and three hours when the high-speed train is in service.

Passenger traffic expected in the year 2000 between the two countries is forty five million divided amongst all the means of transport.

Papa, l'ordinateur et moi

On connaît enfin le profil de l'Homo informaticus moyen. C'est un petit garçon qui s'est fait offrir pour Noël un micro-ordinateur à bas prix et qui y pianote cinquante minutes par jour, six jours par mois, pour lutter contre des météorites en folie. Telles sont en substance les conclusions auxquelles ont abouti les enquêteurs de la Fnac* en sondant leurs clients.

Les chiffres révélés la semaine dernière parlent d'eux-mêmes. Scénario modèle: papa (90% des acheteurs sont des hommes), influencé par ses copains, se décide à offrir un micro-ordinateur à son rejeton. Papa est en général un cadre au niveau d'instruction universitaire. Il hésite peu, ne l'essaie pas et prend en général le moins cher (le prix est pour 67% des gens le premier critère de choix, avant même le nombre de logiciels disponibles et la facilité d'utilisation). Dès qu'il arrive à la maison, papa lit la notice et annonce à tout le monde qu'il a bien l'intention de s'attaquer au basic (47% des acheteurs veulent apprendre à programmer avant l'achat). Mais cette belle ardeur est de courte durée. Papa n'a pas que ça à faire, et les manuels se montrent revêches. Il renonce. Les enfants prennent alors l'ordinateur en main (60% des utilisateurs ont moins de 25 ans, et parmi eux plus de la moitié ont moins de 15 ans). Ils veulent surtout s'amuser avec les logiciels qu'ils ont déjà vus dans les salles de jeux ou chez des amis. (Les programmes ludiques forment 55% des programmes vendus alors que les programmes utilitaires n'en composent que 12%). Ils piratent des cassettes ou des disquettes chez les copains (57%), inventent leurs propres programmes (71%), achètent de nouveaux logiciels (81%).

Cependant, au bout de trois mois, le clavier plastique et le petit téléviseur ont perdu de leur magie. Les parents coriaces, qui étaient restés dans le coup jusque-là, finissent par abandonner, ne laissant qu'un noyau de fidèles irréductibles.

Enfin, toujours selon cette enquête chiffrée, l'ordinateur en s'immisçant dans nos foyers en bouleverserait l'ambiance. Il serait le champion du rapprochement des générations (estiment 55% d'utilisateurs) et (pour 18% de sondés) un sacré semeur de zizanie entre mari et femme . . .

By Bernard Werber, writing in Le Nouvel Observateur, December 1985. © LE NOUVEL OBSERVATEUR.

*Fédération nationale des achats pour cadres

Dad, the computer and me

The profile of the average Homo informaticus is at last known. It is a small boy who has asked to be given an inexpensive micro-computer for Christmas and who taps away at it for fifty minutes a day, six days a month, in order to fight against crazed meteorites. These are, in substance, the conclusions reached by Fnac researchers who carried out a survey among their customers.

The figures revealed last week speak for themselves. Typical scenario: dad (90% of purchasers are men), influenced by his pals, decides to buy a micro-computer for his offspring. Dad is usually an executive with a university education. He barely hesitates, doesn't try it out and generally takes the least expensive one (for 67% of people the price is the most important criterion for choosing a computer, more important even than the amount of software available or ease of use). As soon as he arrives home, dad reads the instructions and announces to everyone that he has every intention of tackling BASIC (47% of purchasers want to learn to program before buying). But this great enthusiasm is of short duration. Dad has other things to do, and the handbooks turn out to be rather daunting. He gives up. The children then take over the computer (60% of users are aged under 25 and, of these, more than half are under 15). They particularly want to play with the software they have already seen in the amusement arcades or at friends' houses. (Computer games form 55% of all programs sold, whilst programs with a practical application account for only 12%). They pirate cassettes or diskettes at their friends' (57%), create their own programs (71%), buy new software (81%).

However, three months later, the plastic keyboard and the small television set have lost some of their magic. Persevering parents, who had participated in everything until then, finally give up, leaving just a small group of devoted enthusiasts.

Finally, again according to the statistics of this survey, it would seem that the computer, by intruding into our homes, upsets the atmosphere. Apparently, it is ideal for bringing the generations closer together (according to 55% of users) and (according to 18% of those interviewed) it is a constant source of friction (lit. 'a right sower of discord') between husband and wife . . .

Key to Exercises

Exercise 1: 1 le passeport. 2 l'hôtel. 3 la valise. 4 une station. 5 un magnétophone. 6 un chéquier. 7 une personne. 8 les journalistes. 9 les prix. 10 de la bière. 11 du vin. 12 des cassettes. 13 des journaux. 14 des autobus.

Exercise 2: 1 Oui, elle a un journal. 2 Oui, ils ont une voiture. 3 Oui, j'ai une radio. 4 Oui, j'ai une carte. 5 Oui, nous avons une clé. 6 Oui, vous avez un disque.

Exercise 3: 1 Non, je n'ai pas de valise. 2 Non, je n'ai pas de passeport. 3 Non, nous n'avons pas de vin. 4 Non, nous n'avons pas de livre. 5 Non, il n'a pas de disques. 6 Non, elle n'a pas de radio. 7 Non, vous n'avez pas de journaux. 8 Non, elles n'ont pas d'appareil-photo.

Exercise 4: 1 J'ai un magnétophone. 2 Je n'ai pas de clés. 3 Nous avons une valise. 4 Elle a de l'alcool. 5 Il n'a pas de journal. 6 Ils ont des cassettes. 7 Elles n'ont pas de cartes. 8 Vous n'avez pas de chéquier. 9 Avez-vous un appareil-photo? 10 Avez-vous des disques? 11 Avez-vous des livres? 12 Avez-vous une radio?

LESSON 2

Exercise 5: 1 Je suis médecin. 2 Il est pilote. 3 Elle est journaliste. 4 Nous sommes banquiers. 5 Vous êtes avocat. 6 Elles sont hôtesses de l'air. 7 Ils sont astronautes.

Exercise 6: 1 Le banquier est pauvre. 2 La secrétaire est stupide. 3 Les médecins sont malheureux. 4 Les journaux sont ennuyeux. 5 Le vin est mauvais. 6 Le livre est difficile. 7 L'hôtesse de l'air est impolie. 8 La bière est bonne.

Exercise 7: 1 Nous habitons à Versailles. 2 Elle travaille à Nice. 3 Il voyage. 4 Je parle deux langues. 5 Elles pratiquent un sport. 6 Ils regardent la télévision. 7 Vous écoutez la radio. 8 Nous préparons une enquête.

Exercise 8: 1 Est-ce que vous téléphonez à l'hôtel? 2 Est-ce que vous réservez une chambre? 3 Est-ce que vous invitez le directeur à dîner? 4 Elle est intelligente? 5 Elle est intéressante? 6 Elle est grande? 7 Exporte-t-il des ordinateurs en France? 8 Importe-t-il des voitures? 9 Vote-t-il pour le premier ministre?

Exercise 9: a) neuf b) deux c) douze d) cinq e) quinze f) douze g) quatorze h) trois.
1 Le premier ministre habite dix Downing Street. 2 James Bond, agent secret zéro zéro sept. 3 La date de la prise de la Bastille: le quatorze juillet. 4 Les Trois Mousquetaires sont finalement quatre. 5 Il y a douze pays dans le Marché commun.

LESSON 3

Exercise 10: 1 Je finis le rapport. 2 Nous garantissons le magnétoscope. 3 Elle choisit un gâteau. 4 Il grossit. 5 Elles maigrissent. 6 Ils remplissent les verres. 7 Nous saisissons l'occasion.

Exercise 11: 1 Ce train est rapide. 2 Cette gare est importante. 3 Ce guichet est fermé. 4 Cette voiture est chère. 5 Cet ascenseur est plein. 6 Ces places sont réservées. 7 Ces compartiments sont occupés. 8 Ces billets son valables.

Exercise 12: 1 J'ai soif. 2 Il a tort. 3 Elle a froid. 4 Nous avons faim. 5 Ils ont raison. 6 Elles ont chaud.

Exercise 13: 1 Non, je ne travaille pas. 2 Non, je n'écoute pas. 3 Non, je n'ai pas faim. 4 Non, je ne choisis jamais de fromage. 5 Non, je ne téléphone jamais. 6 Non, je n'ai jamais froid. 7 Non, il ne mange rien. 8 Non, elle ne prépare rien. 9 Non, il n'exporte rien. 10 Non, nous n'invitons personne. 11 Non, nous ne choisissons personne. 12 Non, nous ne rencontrons personne. 13 Non, ils n'ont plus de voiture. 14 Non, elles n'habitent plus à Paris. 15 Non, elles ne travaillent plus.

Exercise 14: 1 Où travaillez-vous? 2 Quand regardez-vous le film? 3 Comment allez-vous? 4 Qui téléphone? 5 Qui cherchent-ils? 6 Pourquoi mangez-vous? 7 Quelles langues parlez-vous? 8 Combien de cassettes avez-vous? 9 Combien coûte ce journal? 10 Qu'est-ce que vous exportez?

Exercise 15: 1 Réservez deux chambres. 2 Cherchez François. 3 Saisissez l'occasion. 4 Choisissez la méthode Hugo. 5 Montez les bagages. 6 Ne mangez pas trop. 7 Ne grossissez pas. 8 Ne fumez pas. 9 Parlons français. 10 Écoutons la radio. 11 Finissons le rapport.

LESSON 4

Exercise 16: 1 J'ai habité en France. 2 J'ai travaillé en Italie. 3 J'ai réservé les chambres. 4 Elle a écouté la radio. 5 Elle a regardé la télévision. 6 Elle a préparé le rapport. 7 Il a grossi. 8 Il a choisi le fromage. 9 Il a fini le livre. 10 Nous avons copié le document. 11 Nous avons acheté la voiture. 12 Nous avons téléphoné. 13 Vous avez garanti le magnétophone. 14 Vous avez saisi l'occasion. 15 Vous avez invité le premier ministre. 16 Ils ont maigri. 17 Elles ont dépensé 15 francs. 18 Elles ont traversé la Manche.

Exercise 17: 1 Non, je n'ai pas réservé la chambre. 2 Non, je n'ai pas écouté le disque. 3 Non, il n'a pas regardé le film. 4 Non, elle n'a pas préparé le document. 5 Non, nous n'avons pas fini. 6 Non, ils n'ont pas choisi. 7 Non, elles n'ont pas mangé.

Exercise 18: 1 Votre premier vol. 2 Attachez votre ceinture de sécurité. 3 Où sont nos billets? 4 Voici son passeport. 5 Voici sa place. 6 Leurs valises sont dans l'avion. 7 Notre horaire est important. 8 Où sont mes journaux?

Exercise 19: 1 C'est ennuyeux. 2 C'est mauvais. 3 C'est impossible. 4 C'est difficile. 5 C'est affreux. 6 C'est tôt.

Exercise 20: 1 Il est deux heures et quart. 2 Il est quatre heures et demie. 3 Il est six heures. 4 Il est huit heures vingt. 5 Le train arrive à dix heures et quart. 6 Le car arrive à midi moins le quart (or minuit moins le quart). 7 Le bateau part à midi vingt-cinq. 8 L'aéroglisseur part à une heure moins le quart. 9 Le président arrive à neuf heures et quart. 10 La conférence de presse est à dix heures et quart.

Exercise 21: 1 Le premier janvier. 2 Le quatorze février. 3 Le vingt et un mars. 4 Le premier avril. 5 Le premier mai. 6 Le six juin. 7 Le quatorze juillet. 8 Le premier août. 9 Le vingt-trois septembre. 10 Le vingt-cinq octobre/le sept novembre. 11 Le cinq novembre. 12 Le vingt-cinq décembre.

Exercise 22: 1 J'ai travaillé lundi. 2 J'ai écouté la radio mardi. 3 J'ai regardé la télévision mercredi. 4 J'ai fini le rapport jeudi. 5 J'ai acheté un disque vendredi. 6 J'ai téléphoné à ma femme samedi. 7 J'ai parlé espagnol dimanche. 8 Je travaille le lundi. 9 Elle écoute la radio le mardi. 10 Nous regardons la télévision le mercredi.

LESSON 5

Exercise 23: 1 Je vends ma voiture. 2 Il attend sa femme. 3 Nous rendons soixante francs. 4 Cela dépend de mes parents. 5 Est-ce qu'elles entendent la musique? 6 Elle a vendu sa maison. 7 Nous n'avons pas répondu. 8 Avez-vous descendu les bagages? 9 Attends-tu ton frère? 10 As-tu perdu ta mère?

Exercise 24: 1 Est-ce que vous avez pris le train? 2 J'ai appris le français. 3 Apprenez-vous la langue? 4 Comprenez-vous? 5 Tu as souvent surpris ton professeur?

Exercise 25: 1 J'ai mis une annonce dans le journal. 2 Il a permis à sa secrétaire de partir tôt. 3 Vous avez promis de répondre à la lettre? 4 Elle a soumis le rapport ce matin. 5 Mettez-vous le dictionnaire dans la valise? 6 Permettent-ils à leurs enfants de rentrer tard? 7 Nous promettons de parler français. 8 Soumettez-vous déjà le projet?

Exercise 26: 1 rapidement. 2 facilement. 3 finalement. 4 heureusement. 5 attentivement. 6 lentement. 7 complètement. 8 normalement. 9 principalement. 10 temporairement.

Exercise 27: 1 Le rapport? Il est très important. 2 La bière? Elle est mauvaise. 3 La poche? Elle est pleine. 4 La machine? Elle est excellente. 5 Le restaurant? Il est fermé. 6 La qualité? Elle est très bonne. 7 Les produits? Ils sont français. 8 Les messages? Ils sont en anglais. 9 L'explication? Elle n'est pas claire. 10 Le répondeur automatique? Il n'est pas cher.

Exercise 28: 1 Oui, elle vous cherche. 2 Oui, elle me consulte. 3 Oui, je le rencontre. 4 Oui, je la copie. 5 Oui, il l'invite. 6 Oui, il les exporte. 7 Oui, nous le comprenons. 8 Oui, nous la branchons. 9 Oui, nous le mettons en marche. 10 Oui, nous le copions. 11 Oui, elles nous répondent en français. 12 Oui, ils lui téléphonent. 13 Oui, ils lui téléphonent. 14 Oui, ils leur téléphonent. 15 Oui, je lui parle. 16 Oui, je leur réponds. 17 Oui, je leur défends de rentrer tard.

Exercise 29: 1 Oui, je l'ai invité. 2 Oui, je l'ai invitée. 3 Oui, je les ai invités. 4 Oui, il les a exportées. 5 Oui, elle l'a consulté. 6 Oui, elle l'a consultée. 7 Oui, elle les a consultés. 8 Oui, ils l'ont branchée. 9 Oui, ils les ont réservées. 10 Oui, ils l'ont perdue. 11 Oui, nous l'avons compris. 12 Oui, nous l'avons comprise. 13 Oui, nous les avons comprises. 14 Oui, nous les avons compris. 15 Oui, je l'ai mise dans ma poche.

LESSON 6

Exercise 30: 1 Il y a une serviette sur la table. 2 Il y a un taxi devant l'hôtel. 3 Il y a un restaurant derrière l'église. 4 Il y a un supermarché à côté de la banque. 5 Il y a une librairie en face de l'université. 6 Est-ce qu'il y a une cabine téléphonique près de la gare? 7 Est-ce qu'il y a des livres anglais à la bibliothèque? 8 Est-ce qu'il y a un tunnel sous la Manche? 9 Je vais au cinéma. 10 Elle va aux États-Unis. 11 Avez-vous le numéro de téléphone du théâtre? 12 J'ai acheté un journal pour mon ami(e). 13 Elle apprend le français avec des cassettes. 14 C'est difficile de travailler sans ma secrétaire. 15 Mangeons après le spectacle. 16 Téléphonons avant 9 heures.

Exercise 31: 1 Le banquier est plus riche que le professeur. 2 Le facteur est plus pauvre que l'avocat. 3 L'hôtesse de l'air est plus belle que l'actrice. 4 La lettre est moins importante que le télégramme. 5 Le pilote est aussi courageux que l'astronaute. 6 Le français n'est pas si difficile que le russe. 7 Elle parle plus distinctement que Paul. 8 Il écoute plus attentivement que son frère.

Exercise 32: 1 Oui, c'est le restaurant le plus chic du monde. 2 Oui, c'est la plus grande librairie du monde. 3 Oui, c'est le magasin le plus célèbre du monde. 4 Oui, c'est la plus belle cathédrale du monde. 5 Oui, c'est la meilleure bière du monde. 6 Oui, c'est le parc le plus agréable du monde. 7 Oui, c'est la ville la plus intéressante du monde. 8 Oui, c'est la voiture la plus confortable du monde. 9 Oui, c'est l'avion le plus impressionnant du monde.

Exercise 33: 1 Il pleut. 2 Il fait du brouillard. 3 Il fait du vent. 4 Il fait froid. 5 Il fait du soleil. 6 Il neige. 7 Il fait chaud. 8 Il fait mauvais. 9 Il fait beau.

Exercise 34:
A. 1 Je suis médecin. 2 Ce matin je suis arrivé à l'hôpital à 7 heures. 3 Je suis allé à une réunion à 10 heures. 4 Je suis parti avec deux infirmières.
B. 1 Je suis journaliste. 2 Hier je suis allée à une conférence de presse. 3 Je suis montée au restaurant à une heure. 4 Je suis retournée au bureau très tard.
C. 1 Nicole et Sophie sont étudiantes. 2 Ce matin elles sont allées à l'université à 9 heures. 3 Elles sont restées toute la journée à la bibliothèque. 4 Elles sont revenues à la maison à 5 heures.

Exercise 35: 1 Les ingénieurs sont arrivés hier. 2 Les actrices sont

déjà parties. 3 Nous sommes revenues tôt. 4 Tu es descendu.
5 Est-ce que l'infirmière est restée toute la journée? 6 Êtes-vous
revenu très tard?

Exercise 36: 1 Je voudrais une carte postale. 2 Je voudrais un
timbre. 3 Je voudrais un plan de la ville. 4 Je voudrais un journal
anglais. 5 Je voudrais du lait. 6 Je voudrais du sucre. 7 Je voudrais
du thé. 8 Je voudrais téléphoner à Londres. 9 Je voudrais envoyer un
télégramme. 10 Je voudrais régler la note.

Exercise 37: 1 Il me faut un crayon. 2 Il me faut un stylo-bille. 3 Il
lui faut une gomme. 4 Il lui faut du papier à lettres. 5 Il leur faut des
enveloppes. 6 Il leur faut des cigarettes. 7 Il leur faut des allumettes.

LESSON 7

Exercise 38: 1 Non, j'ai beaucoup de cravates. 2 Non, j'ai beaucoup
de mouchoirs. 3 Non, j'ai beaucoup de robes. 4 Oui, il a maintenant
trop de pantalons. 5 Oui, elle a maintenant trop de jupes. 6 Oui, elle
a maintenant trop de foulards. 7 Il a peu de patience. 8 Avez-vous (or
as-tu) mis assez de chemises de nuit dans la valise? 9 J'ai plus de
cardigans que Monique. 10 Vous avez moins de costumes que Pierre.

Exercise 39: 1 Je vais écouter la radio. 2 Je vais acheter un journal.
3 Je vais étudier le français. 4 Je vais faire mes courses. 5 Il réparera
la voiture. 6 Il jouera au tennis. 7 Il écrira une lettre. 8 Il visitera le
musée. 9 Ils tapisseront l'appartement. 10 Ils organiseront une
réunion. 11 Ils iront à une conférence internationale. 12 Ils
passeront un week-end à Londres. 13 Elle finira sa lettre. 14 Nous
irons au théâtre la semaine prochaine. 15 Vous surprendrez votre
père. 16 Tu choisiras ta robe le mois prochain.

Exercise 40: 1 Je peux acheter les légumes au marché. 2 Je peux
préparer le rapport. 3 Nous ne pouvons pas arriver lundi. 4 Nous ne
pouvons pas lire son écriture. 5 Elle doit signer le contrat. 6 Elle doit
arrêter de fumer. 7 Ils ne doivent pas décourager les étudiants. 8 Ils
ne doivent pas garer la voiture devant l'hôpital. 9 Il veut faire le tour
du monde. 10 Il veut dépenser moins d'argent. 11 Savez-vous (or
sais-tu) conduire? 12 Savez-vous (or sais-tu) nager?

Exercise 41: 1 L'Allemagne (*f*). 2 La Belgique. 3 Le Danemark.
4 L'Espagne (*f*). 5 La France. 6 La Grèce. 7 La Hollande.
8 L'Italie (*f*). 9 Le Luxembourg. 10 Le Portugal. 11 La République
d'Irlande. 12 Le Royaume-Uni.

Exercise 42: 1 Nous passons nos vacances en Grèce. 2 Avez-vous l'intention d'aller au Japon? 3 La Grande-Bretagne exporte des voitures en France. 4 Est-ce que le diplomate est arrivé en Russie?

Exercise 43: a) Vingt. b) Vingt-deux. c) Trente et un. d) Quarante-sept. e) Cinquante-neuf. f) Soixante et un. g) Soixante-dix. h) Soixante-dix-neuf. i) Quatre-vingt-un. j) Quatre-vingt-onze. k) Quatre-vingt-dix-neuf. l) Cent.

LESSON 8

Exercise 44: 1 Il jouait au football. 2 Il allait à la pêche. 3 Il collectionnait des timbres. 4 Elle chantait. 5 Elle écoutait des disques. 6 Nous apprenions l'espagnol. 7 Nous habitions dans une petite maison. 8 Nous faisions de la photo(graphie). 9 Je finissais la traduction quand j'ai entendu un bruit en haut. 10 Elle faisait les courses quand elle a perdu son porte-monnaie. 11 Ils regardaient la télévision quand le cambrioleur est entré dans la maison.

Exercise 45: 1 L'hôtel, que vous cherchez, est à droite. 2 Je voudrais la chambre qui donne sur le parc. 3 La chambre, que nous avons réservée pour vous, est à côté de l'ascenseur. 4 J'ai apporté le petit déjeuner que votre mari a commandé. 5 Où est le poste de télévision qui ne marche pas? 6 Les valises, qui sont dans le vestibule, sont très lourdes. 7 La réceptionniste, à qui vous avez parlé, est bilingue. 8 Le client, dont le fils est malade, est dans la chambre 5. 9 N'avez-vous pas compris ce que la femme de chambre vous a dit? 10 La note, que vous avez préparée, est correcte.

Exercise 46: 1 Si j'étais riche, je ferais le tour du monde. 2 Si je ne travaillais pas, je peindrais et je dessinerais. 3 S'il avait beaucoup de temps, il apprendrait le portugais. 4 Si elle parlait français, elle travaillerait comme interprète. 5 Si elle parlait allemand, elle travaillerait comme secrétaire bilingue. 6 Si vous étiez marié, vous rentreriez plus tôt le soir à la maison. 7 S'ils étaient en chômage, ils chercheraient du travail. 8 Si elles avaient des enfants, elles resteraient à la maison. 9 Si j'avais le temps, je lirais beaucoup. 10 Si nous voulions maigrir, nous mangerions moins et ferions de la gymnastique.

Exercise 47: 1 . . . avec lui. 2 . . . à côté d'elle. 3 . . . sans eux. 4 . . . qu'elles. 5 . . . que lui. 6 . . . Elle. 7 Ce sont (or C'est) eux qui . . .

Exercise 48: 1 Je ne sais pas si Paul a fini son travail. 2 Je ne connais pas les Dupont. 3 Savez-vous où je peux louer une machine à écrire? 4 Savez-vous si le médecin est libre? 5 Est-ce que Marie-Claude connaît ma tante?

Exercise 49: 1 Je ne vous dérange pas. Je pensais justement à vous. Vous n'êtes pas trop occupée? . . . quand vous avez frappé à la porte. À qui est-ce que vous écriviez? À propos, comment va votre travail? Qu'est-ce que vous feriez de tout ce temps libre? Vous feriez mieux de prendre votre retraite tout de suite.

LESSON 9

Exercise 50: 1 Mon rhume est pire que celui de ma soeur. 2 Cet hôpital est plus moderne que celui que la Princesse a visité l'année dernière. 3 Quel chirurgien a effectué la greffe du coeur? Celui-ci ou celui-là? 4 Avez-vous rendez-vous (or un rendez-vous) avec ce dentiste-ci ou celui-là? 5 Le (la) kinésithérapeute m'a donné ceci. 6 Le pharmacien a préparé cela. 7 C'est votre nouvelle secrétaire. 8 Ce sont vos malades.

Exercise 51: 1 Le barman vous a servi votre whisky, mais où est le mien? 2 Mon poisson est délicieux; le vôtre n'est pas frais. 3 J'ai payé notre addition et ils ont payé la leur. 4 Est-ce que ce chapeau est à vous ou à votre ami? 5 Avec quoi voulez-vous manger ce repas chinois? Avec des baguettes? Quoi? Non! Avec un couteau et une fourchette. 6 Quel est le numéro de téléphone du restaurant italien? 7 Quels légumes a-t-elle commandés? 8 Qu'est-ce qui sent si bon? 9 Voici une liste des meilleurs restaurants de Paris; lequel préférez-vous? 10 A qui est cette cuillère?

Exercise 52: 1 Elle tape lentement à la machine. 2 Ils chantent mal. 3 Ne parlez pas si bas. 4 Il va souvent chez ses parents. 5 Nous avons déjà mangé. 6 Il va sûrement pleuvoir ou neiger. 7 Elle prend un bain en bas. 8 Elles ont fait les courses hier.

LESSON 10

Exercise 53: 1 Il se réveille à 7 heures du matin. 2 Il se lave. 3 Il se rase. 4 Il va au travail. 5 Elle se lève à 8 heures du matin. 6 Elle prend une douche. 7 Elle se peigne. 8 Elle se maquille. 9 Elle va à la gare. 10 Nous nous lavons. 11 Nous nous habillons vite. 12 Nous nous promenons. 13 Nous nous couchons à dix heures du soir. 14 Je me suis amusée. 15 Vous ne vous êtes pas trompée. 16 Elles se reposent. 17 Ils ont lavé la voiture eux-mêmes. 18 Nous nous brossons les dents chaque matin.

Exercise 54: 1 Il a quitté la maison sans dire un mot. 2 Elle est habituée à écouter des disques dans sa chambre. 3 Avant de réparer la lampe, il a téléphoné à l'électricien. 4 Après avoir préparé le petit déjeuner, elle a fait le ménage. 5 Ma mère a commencé par dire que toute la famille était en bonne santé et a fini par souhaiter à tout le monde une bonne année. 6 Ce poste de radio est excellent pour capter les émissions françaises.

Exercise 55: 1 J'ai l'intention d'acheter des lunettes de soleil. 2 Sera-t-il possible de faire des excursions? 3 Nous préférons louer un appartement. 4 Ils m'ont invitée à aller à la pêche. 5 J'hésite à faire du ski nautique. 6 Aurez-vous l'occasion de faire de la planche à voile?

Exercise 56: 1 Est-ce-que vous me l'avez donné? 2 Il nous les a promises. 3 Il a l'intention de me les vendre. 4 Je le lui ai envoyé. 5 Il la lui montre. 6 Nous les leur avons données.

LESSON 11

Exercise 57: 1 Comme (or puisque) l'ami de Paul vient camper avec nous, nous devrons acheter un lit de camp supplémentaire. 2 Quand vous saurez parler français, nous irons faire du camping en France. 3 Saisissez-vous chaque occasion pour parler français, quand vous êtes en Belgique? 4 Je n'aime pas ce camping parce qu'il n'y a pas de piscine. 5 Nous sommes quatre mais nous avons seulement (or nous n'avons que) trois sacs de couchage. 6 La voiture est tombée en panne, donc nous avons décidé de camper dans un champ.

Exercise 58: a) deux cent cinquante b) trois cents c) quatre cent trente d) cinq cent soixante-dix e) six cent quatre-vingts f) mille quatre cent quarante.

Exercise 59: 1 la première discothèque 2 le deuxième (second) casino 3 la troisième boîte de nuit 4 le quatrième théâtre 5 le cinquième concert 6 le sixième opéra 7 le septième cinéma 8 la huitième patinoire 9 le neuvième ballet 10 le dixième restaurant.

Exercise 60: 1 L'importance de la décision a été soulignée par le président de la République française. 2 La Grande-Bretagne sera reliée au continent par un tunnel ferroviaire en 1993. 3 Un lien routier sera construit plus tard. 4 Cette décision historique a été annoncée à Lille. 5 Les touristes étrangers ont souvent été découragés par la traversée de la Manche.

Exercise 61: 1 Elle s'est cassé le bras en faisant du ski. 2 Je suis tombé en patinant. 3 En allant aux cours du soir trois fois par semaine, il a obtenu son diplôme. 4 Voyant que l'automobiliste était blessé, l'agent de police a appelé une ambulance. 5 En téléphonant, vous aurez la réponse tout de suite.

Exercise 62: 1 Téléphonez-lui – non, ne lui téléphonez pas. 2 Envoyez-leur cette brochure – non, ne la leur envoyez pas. 3 Copiez ce document – non, ne le copiez pas. 4 Donnez-moi le catalogue – non, ne me le donnez pas. 5 Envoyez-lui les échantillons – non, ne les lui envoyez pas. 6 Tapez cette lettre – non, ne la tapez pas. 7 Soyez ici à 9 heures – non, à 8 heures. 8 Voulez-vous bien faire des heures supplémentaires?

Exercise 63: 1 Je suis marié depuis cinq ans. 2 J'habite dans cette maison depuis quatre ans. 3 Je travaille pour cette banque depuis trois ans. 4 J'ai cette voiture depuis deux ans. 5 J'apprends à jouer du piano depuis un an.

Exercise 64: 1 Mais je viens d'appeler un docteur. 2 Mais je viens de prévenir les pompiers. 3 Mais je viens de vous montrer mon permis de conduire. 4 Mais les ambulanciers viennent de transporter les blessés à l'hôpital. 5 Mais je viens de vous donner mon adresse.

LESSON 12

Exercise 65: 1 Qu'est-ce que vous faites dans la vie? 2 Ma soeur fait une tarte aux pommes. 3 Je vais faire une conférence sur la psychologie devant 200 personnes. 4 Elle a fait une promenade au parc hier. 5 Il fait de la fièvre. 6 Ne fais pas l'idiot. 7 J'ai fait travailler mon fils. 8 Je me fais construire une maison à Avignon.

Exercise 66: 1 he gave 2 I sold 3 we finished 4 she had 5 I was 6 you had 7 he took 8 she went out 9 they read 10 they put.

Exercise 67: 1 Je suggère que le président fasse une déclaration à la télévision. 2 Il faut que nous continuions notre conquête de l'espace. 3 Il voudrait que le lancement du vaisseau spatial ait lieu la semaine prochaine. 4 Je suis content que vous participiez à cette mission spatiale. 5 Il est important que le lancement soit filmé en direct. 6 À moins que vous ne puissiez me donner toutes les données enregistrées par les ordinateurs, je ne peux pas prendre de décision. 7 Nous sommes contents que le président ait décidé de reporter son discours. 8 Bien que les astronautes soient habitués à l'apesanteur, ils ont quand même un peu de mal à mener leurs expériences à bord du vaisseau spatial.

Mini-dictionary

Although the following is not an exhaustive list of words found in the book, it will be helpful as a quick reference. Numbers against some entries indicate lessons and sections where irregular verbs and other important points are explained. See sections 23–26 for seasons, months of the year, dates and days of the week.

able, to be able pouvoir *sec. 48*
above au-dessus de
abroad à l'étranger
actress actrice
address adresse (*f*)
advance, in advance à l'avance
advertisement annonce (*f*)
advertising publicité (*f*)
advise conseiller
after après
afternoon après-midi (*m* or *f*)
afterwards ensuite
again encore
agency agence (*f*)
ago il y a
air hostess hôtesse de l'air
airline company compagnie (*f*) aérienne
alcohol alcool (*m*)
all tout *page 75*
allow permettre (*irreg*) *sec. 30*
already déjà
also aussi
although bien que, quoique
always toujours
ambulance ambulance (*f*)
ambulance driver ambulancier (*m*), -ière (*f*)
America Amérique (*f*)
American américain
analyse analyser
and et
announce annoncer *sec. 81*
answer (*vb*) répondre

apple pomme (*f*)
appointment rendez-vous (*m*)
appreciate apprécier
approve (of) approuver
arm bras (*m*)
armchair fauteuil (*m*)
arrive arriver
ask (for) demander
astronaut astronaute (*m* & *f*)
attach attacher
aunt tante
avoid éviter

bad mauvais
badly mal
baker's boulangerie (*f*)
ball-point pen stylo-bille (*m*)
bank banque (*f*)
banker banquier (*m*)
bar bar (*m*)
bath bain (*m*)
be, to be être (*irreg*) *sec. 6*
beach plage (*f*)
beautiful beau *less. 6*
because parce que
bed lit (*m*)
  to go to bed se coucher
bedroom chambre (*f*)
beer bière (*f*)
before avant
begin commencer *sec. 81*
behind derrière
Belgium Belgique (*f*)
better meilleur, mieux

between entre
big grand
bilingual bilingue
bill addition, note, (f)
blood pressure tension (f)
blue bleu
boat bateau (m)
book livre (m)
bookshop librairie (f)
boring ennuyeux
    to be bored s'ennuyer *sec. 81*
boss patron (m),-onne (f)
bottle bouteille (f)
brand marque (f)
brave courageux
bread pain (m)
break (*vb*) casser
breakdown panne (f)
break down tomber en panne
breakfast petit déjeuner (m)
briefcase serviette (f)
bring apporter, amener *sec. 81*
bring down descendre
bring up monter
Britain Grande-Bretagne (f)
British britannique
broadcast émission (f)
brochure brochure (f)
brother frère
brown brun
build construire (*irreg*) *page 140*
burglar cambrioleur (m)
burn (*vb*) brûler
bus autobus (m)
business affaires (*f.pl*)
businessman homme d'affaires
busy occupé
but mais
butcher's boucherie (f)
buy acheter *sec. 81*

cake gâteau (m)
call (*vb*) appeler, *sec. 81*
    to be called s'appeler
camera appareil-photo (m)

camp (*vb*) camper
can (to be able) pouvoir (*irreg.*) *sec. 48*
Canada Canada (m)
cancel annuler
car voiture (f)
card carte (f)
cashdesk caisse (f)
castle château (m)
cathedral cathédrale (f)
chambermaid femme de chambre
change (*vb*) changer *sec. 81*
Channel Manche (f)
check (*vb*) vérifier
cheese fromage (m)
chemist's pharmacie (f)
cheque chèque (m)
China Chine (f)
choose choisir
church église (f)
clean (*vb*) nettoyer *sec. 81*
client client (m),-e (f)
close (*vb*) fermer
clothes vêtements (*m.pl*)
coach car (m)
coffee café (m)
cold froid
    to be cold avoir froid
colour couleur (f)
come venir (*irreg*) *page 74*
comfortable confortable
Common Market Marché commun (m)
computer ordinateur (m)
conference conférence (f)
congratulate féliciter
consult consulter
continue continuer
contract contrat (m)
copy (*vb*) copier
correct (*vb*) corriger *sec. 81*
cost (*vb*) coûter
country pays (m)
create créer
credit card carte (f) de crédit

criticise critiquer
cross (*vb*) traverser
cup tasse (*f*)
customs douane (*f*)
cut (*vb*) couper

dangerous dangereux
date date (*f*); rendez-vous (*m*)
daughter fille
dear cher
decide décider
deckchair chaise (*f*) longue
delicious délicieux
dentist dentiste (*m* & *f*)
departure départ (*m*)
dictionary dictionnaire (*m*)
diet régime (*m*)
difficult difficile
dinner dîner (*m*)
director directeur (*m*),-trice (*f*)
disco discothèque (*f*)
discourage décourager *sec. 81*
dish plat (*m*)
disturb déranger *sec. 81*
do faire (*irreg*) *sec. 77*
doctor médecin, docteur (*m*)
doubt (*vb*) douter
downstairs en bas
dreadful affreux
dress robe (*f*)
drink (*vb*) boire (*irreg*) *page 92*
drive (*vb*) conduire (*irreg*) *less. 7*,
    rouler
driving licence permis (*m*) de
    conduire

each chaque
early tôt
easy facile
eat manger *sec. 81*
electrician électricien (*m*)
embassy ambassade (*f*)
encourage encourager *sec. 81*
end fin (*f*)
engine moteur (*m*)

engineer ingénieur (*m*)
England Angleterre (*f*)
English anglais
enjoy oneself s'amuser
enough assez
enter entrer
envelope enveloppe (*f*)
especially surtout
even même
evening soir (*m*)
everyone tout le monde
everything tout
everywhere partout
exactly exactement
excellent excellent
excursion excursion (*f*)
expensive cher
explanation explication (*f*)
export exporter
extra supplément (*m*)

fall (*vb*) tomber
family famille (*f*)
famous célèbre
far loin
fashion mode (*f*)
fast rapide
father père
fever fièvre (*f*)
field champ (*m*)
fill remplir
find trouver
fine beau; bien
finish (*vb*) finir
fireman pompier
first premier
fish poisson (*m*)
fishing pêche (*f*)
    to go fishing aller à la pêche
fishmonger's poissonnerie (*f*)
flat appartement (*m*)
flight vol (*m*)
fog brouillard (*m*)
food nourriture (*f*)
for pour

forbid défendre
foreign étranger
forget oublier
fork fourchette (*f*)
fortunately heureusement
free libre
French français
fresh frais, fraîche (*f*)
friend ami (*m*),-e (*f*)
from de
front
  in front of devant
fruit fruit(s) (*m*)
full plein

garage garage (*m*)
generally généralement
German allemand
Germany Allemagne (*f*)
get obtenir (*irreg*) *page 132*
get up se lever *sec. 81*
give donner
give back rendre
glass verre (*m*)
glove gant (*m*)
go aller (*irreg*) *page 74*
go down descendre
go out sortir (*irreg*) *page 132*
go up monter
good bon, bonne (*f*)
goodbye au revoir
government gouvernement (*m*)
Great Britain Grande-Bretagne (*f*)
Greece Grèce (*f*)
grey gris
grocer's épicerie (*f*)
group groupe (*m*)
guarantee (*vb*) garantir
guide guide (*m*)
guide book guide (*m*)

hair cheveux (*m.pl*)
hairdresser coiffeur (*m*), -euse (*f*)
hall vestibule (*m*)
ham jambon (*m*)

hand main (*f*)
handkerchief mouchoir (*m*)
handwriting écriture (*f*)
happy heureux
hat chapeau (*m*)
have avoir (*irreg*) *sec. 4*
have to (must) devoir (*irreg*) *sec. 48*
head tête (*f*)
health santé (*f*)
hear entendre
heart coeur (*m*)
heavy lourd
help (*vb*) aider
her *sec. 19, 33, 54*
hers *sec. 57*
here ici
here is voici
hire louer
his *sec. 19, 57*
holiday vacances (*f.pl*)
hope (*vb*) espérer *sec. 81*
hospital hôpital (*m*)
hot chaud
hotel hôtel (*m*)
house maison (*f*)
hovercraft aéroglisseur (*m*)
how comment
how much, how many combien
hungry, to be hungry avoir faim
hurry se dépêcher
husband mari

ice cream glace (*f*)
ill malade
immediately tout de suite
import importer
important important
impossible impossible
impressive impressionnant
improve améliorer
included compris
increase augmentation (*f*)
information renseignement(s) (*m*)
injured blessé
interesting intéressant

interpreter interprète (*m* & *f*)
invite inviter
invoice facture (*f*)
Ireland Irlande (*f*)
Irish irlandais

jacket veste (*f*)
jam confiture (*f*)
Japan Japon (*m*)
Japanese japonais
journalist journaliste (*m* & *f*)

key clé (*f*)
knife couteau (*m*)
knock (*vb*) frapper
know savoir (*irreg*) *sec. 48,*
    connaître (*irreg*) *sec. 55*

lady dame
lamp lampe (*f*)
language langue (*f*)
large grand
last dernier
late en retard
lawyer avocat (*m*),-e (*f*)
learn apprendre (*irreg*) *sec. 29*
leave (*vb*) partir (*irreg*) *page 46,*
    quitter
lecture conférence (*f*)
left: on/to the left à gauche
leg jambe (*f*)
less moins
lesson leçon (*f*)
letter lettre (*f*)
library bibliothèque (*f*)
life vie (*f*)
lift ascenseur (*m*)
like (*vb*) aimer
listen (to) écouter
live habiter, vivre (*irreg*) *page 147*
long long, longue (*f*)
look (at) regarder
look for chercher
lorry camion (*m*)
lose perdre

loud fort
luck chance (*f*)
luggage bagages (*m.* usu.*pl*)
lunch déjeuner (*m*)

machine appareil (*m*), machine (*f*)
main principal
make faire (*irreg*) *sec. 77*
managing director
    président-directeur général (*m*)
many beaucoup (de)
map carte (*f*), plan (*m*)
market marché (*m*)
    Common Market Marché
    commun (*m*)
marriage mariage (*m*)
married marié
    to get married se marier
match allumette (*f*)
me me, moi
meal repas (*m*)
meat viande (*f*)
mechanic mécanicien (*m*)
medicine médicament (*m*)
meet rencontrer
meeting réunion (*f*)
message message (*m*)
method méthode (*f*)
midday midi (*m*)
midnight minuit (*m*)
milk lait (*m*)
mine *sec. 57*
mistake erreur (*f*)
    to make a mistake se tromper
modern moderne
moment instant, moment (*m*)
money argent (*m*)
month mois (*m*)
mood humeur (*f*)
more plus
morning matin (*m*)
mother mère
motorbike moto (*f*)
motorist automobiliste (*m* & *f*)
motorway autoroute (*f*)

much beaucoup (de)
  as much/many autant (de)
  so much/many tant (de)
museum musée (*m*)
music musique (*f*)
must (to have to) devoir (*irreg*)
  sec. 48
my mon, ma, mes

name nom (*m*)
napkin serviette (*f*)
near près (*adv.*) près de (*prep.*)
necessary nécessaire
need *sec. 45*
nephew neveu
never jamais, ne (*verb*) jamais
new neuf, neuve (*f*), nouveau *sec. 27*
news nouvelle(s) (*f*)
newspaper journal (*m*)
next prochain
next to à côté de
night nuit (*f*)
night club boîte (*f*) de nuit
nightdress chemise (*f*) de nuit
noise bruit (*m*)
noisy bruyant
no non
no longer ne (*verb*) plus
no one personne,
  ne (*verb*) personne
normal normal
nose nez (*m*)
nothing rien, ne (*verb*) rien
now maintenant
number numéro (*m*)
nurse infirmier (*m*),-ière (*f*)

obey obéir
obtain obtenir (*irreg*) *page 132*
obvious évident
occupied occupé
of de
office bureau
often souvent
old vieux, vieille (*f*) *sec. 27*

on sur
only seul, seulement
open (*vb*) ouvrir (*irreg*) j'ouvre,
  nous ouvrons; j'ai ouvert
open ouvert
opera opéra (*m*)
opinion avis (*m*)
  in my opinion à mon avis
opportunity occasion (*f*)
opposite en face (*adv.*), en face de
  (*prep.*)
or ou
order (*vb*) commander
  in order to pour, afin de
ordinary ordinaire
organise organiser
other autre
our notre, nos
ours le/la nôtre, les nôtres
overlook donner sur
overtime heures (*f*) supplémentaires

paint (*vb*) peindre (*irreg*) *page 101*
park parc (*m*)
passport passeport (*m*)
patient malade (*m & f*)
pay (for) payer *sec. 81*
pencil crayon (*m*)
people gens (*m.pl*)
perfect (*vb*) perfectionner
perfume parfum (*m*)
perhaps peut-être
permit (*vb*) permettre (*irreg*) *sec. 30*
persuade persuader
petrol essence (*f*)
pick up (broadcast) capter
pity dommage (*m*)
  what a pity! quel dommage!
plan projet (*m*)
plane avion (*m*)
play (*vb*) jouer
pleasant agréable
please s'il vous plaît
please (*vb*) plaire (*irreg*) *page 118*
pleased content

pleasure plaisir (*m*)
pocket poche (*f*)
policeman agent de police
polite poli
poor pauvre
possible possible
postcard carte (*f*) postale
postman facteur
post office bureau (*m*) de poste
postpone reporter
practise pratiquer
prefer préférer *sec. 81*
prepare préparer
prescription ordonnance (*f*)
press presse (*f*)
press conference conférence (*f*) de
  presse
pretty joli
prevent empêcher
price prix (*m*)
probable probable
product produit (*m*)
profession profession (*f*)
promise (*vb*) promettre (*irreg*) *sec.
  30*
psychology psychologie (*f*)
purse porte-monnaie (*m*)
put mettre (*irreg*) *sec. 30*

quality qualité (*f*)
queen reine
question question (*f*)
queue (*vb*) faire la queue
quick rapide
quickly vite, rapidement

radio radio (*f*)
railway station gare (*f*)
rain (*vb*) pleuvoir (*irreg*)
  it is raining il pleut
  it rained il a plu
rapid rapide
read lire (*irreg*) *page 64*
ready prêt
reason raison (*f*)

reasonable raisonnable
recently récemment
recommend recommander
record disque (*m*)
record player électrophone (*m*)
refuse (*vb*) refuser
regret (*vb*) regretter
remember se souvenir de (*irreg.,
  conj. like venir*) *page 68*
repair (*vb*) réparer
repeat répéter *sec. 81*
reply (*vb*) répondre
reserve réserver
rest (*vb*) se reposer
restaurant restaurant (*m*)
return (*vb*) retourner, rentrer
rich riche
right correct
  on/to the right à droite
  to be right avoir raison
room salle (*f*)
  bedroom chambre (*f*)
Russia Russie (*f*)
Russian russe

sad triste
salad salade (*f*)
salary salaire (*m*)
say dire (*irreg*) *page 92*
Scotland Écosse (*f*)
Scottish écossais
sea mer (*f*)
seat place (*f*)
secretary secrétaire (*m & f*)
see voir (*irreg*) *less. 11*
sell vendre
send envoyer (*irreg*) *page 77*
serious grave
serve servir (*irreg*) *page 114*
settle régler *sec. 81*
several plusieurs
shave (*vb*) raser, se raser
shirt chemise (*f*)
shop magasin (*m*)
shopkeeper commerçant (*m*),-e (*f*)

shopping courses (*f.pl*)
shop window vitrine (*f*)
short court
show spectacle (*m*)
show (*vb*) montrer
shut (*vb*) fermer
sign (*vb*) signer
since depuis; puisque
sing chanter
sister soeur
sit down s'asseoir (*irreg*) *page 132*
size taille (*f*)
skate (*vb*) patiner
skating rink patinoire (*f*)
ski (*vb*) faire du ski
   water-skiing ski (*m*) nautique
skirt jupe (*f*)
sleep (*vb*) dormir (*irreg*) je dors, il
   dort, n. dormons; j'ai dormi
sleeping bag sac (*m*) de couchage
slowly lentement
small petit
smart chic
smoke (*vb*) fumer
snow (*vb*) neiger *sec. 81*
so si; donc
some *sec. 1*
something quelque chose
son fils
soon bientôt
   as soon as aussitôt que
sorry désolé
soup soupe (*f*)
Spain Espagne (*f*)
Spanish espagnol
speak parler
special offer promotion (*f*)
spend (money) dépenser
spend (time) passer
spoon cuillère (*f*)
sport sport (*m*)
square place (*f*)
stamp timbre (*m*)
start (*vb*) commencer *sec. 81*
station gare, station (*f*)

stay (*vb*) rester
still encore, toujours
stop s'arrêter, cesser
straight on tout droit
street rue (*f*)
street map plan (*m*)
student étudiant (*m*),-e (*f*)
study (*vb*) étudier
succeed réussir
sugar sucre (*m*)
suit costume (*m*)
suitcase valise (*f*)
sun soleil (*m*)
sunglasses lunettes (*f*) de soleil
supermarket supermarché (*m*)
surprise (*vb*) surprendre (*irreg*) *sec.*
   29
sure sûr
survey enquête (*f*)
swim nager, se baigner
swimming pool piscine (*f*)

tablet comprimé (*m*)
take prendre (*irreg*) *sec. 29*
   take down descendre
   take part participer
   take place avoir lieu
   take up monter
tall grand
tape recorder magnétophone (*m*)
tea thé (*m*)
telegram télégramme (*m*)
telephone (*vb*) téléphoner
telephone booth cabine (*f*)
   téléphonique
tell dire (*irreg*) *page 92*
tent tente (*f*)
that/this *sec. 12, 56*
their leur, leurs
there là, y
these/those *sec. 12, 56*
think penser
thirsty, to be thirsty avoir soif
ticket billet (*m*)
time temps (*m*); heure (*f*); fois (*f*)

timetable horaire (*m*)
tired fatigué
today aujourd'hui
toilet toilettes (*f.pl*)
tomorrow demain
too trop
too much/many trop (de)
tooth dent (*f*)
towel serviette (*f*)
town ville (*f*)
train train (*m*)
translation traduction (*f*)
travel (*vb*) voyager *sec. 81*
try (*vb*) essayer *sec. 81*
tyre pneu (*m*)

umbrella parapluie (*m*)
under sous
understand comprendre (*irreg*) *sec. 29*
unfortunately malheureusement
United States États-Unis (*m.pl*)
until jusqu'à, jusqu'à ce que
upstairs en haut
usually d'habitude
use (*vb*) utiliser

valid valable
vegetable légume (*m*)
video recorder magnétoscope (*m*)
visit (*vb*) visiter

wait (for) attendre
waiter garçon
waitress serveuse
wake up réveiller, se réveiller
Wales pays (*m*) de Galles
walk (*vb*) marcher

to go for a walk se promener *sec. 81*
wallet porte-feuille (*m*)
want (*vb*) vouloir (*irreg*) *sec. 48*
warm, to be warm avoir chaud
wash (*vb*) laver, se laver
watch (*vb*) regarder
water eau (*f*)
water-skiing ski (*m*) nautique
week semaine (*f*)
well bien
Welsh gallois
what *sec. 15, 58*
wheel roue (*f*)
when quand
where où
which *sec. 15, 52*
who, whom *sec. 15, 52*
why pourquoi
wife femme
wind vent (*m*)
windsurfing planche (*f*) à voile
wine vin (*m*)
wish (*vb*) désirer, souhaiter
wonderful magnifique
word mot (*m*)
work (*vb*) travailler; (*of machines*) marcher
write écrire (*irreg*) *page 85*
writing paper papier (*m*) à lettres
wrong, to be wrong avoir tort

year an (*m*)
yesterday hier
young jeune
your *sec. 19*
yours *sec. 57*

Index

The numbers refer to section headings, unless pages are specified